Crir

Recei

Edited by

Marilyn M

A Series from LFB Scho

Offender Drug Abuse and Recidivism

An Access to Recovery Program

Michael A. Seredycz

LFB Scholarly Publishing LLC
El Paso 2010

Seredycz, Michael A.
Offender drug abuse and recidivism : an access to recovery program / Michael A. Seredycz.
p. cm. -- (Criminal justice: recent scholarship)
Includes bibliographical references and index.
ISBN 978-1-59332-402-5 (hbk. : alk. paper)
1. Recidivism--United States. 2. Criminals--Rehabilitation--United States. 3. Ex-convicts--Drug use--United States. 4. Drug abuse--Treatment--United States. I. Title.
HV6049.S46 2010
364.3'8--dc22
2010019499

ISBN 978-1-59332-402-5

Printed on acid-free 250-year-life paper.

Manufactured in the United States of America.

Table of Contents

List of Tables

Acknowledgments

I would like to dedicate this book to my family and friends from the Universities of North Dakota and Nebraska-Omaha. I thank my mom, dad and brother for their support and guidance. I would also like to extend my sincere thanks to Bill Wakefield and Michael Meyer for their time and effort.

CHAPTER 1:

The Politics of Offender Reentry

The United States criminal justice system has become overburdened due to the moral panic to toughen legislation creating an incarceration explosion of non-violent drug using criminals. Subsequently, this creates more obstacles for offenders trying to reintegrate into their communities after being incarcerated. This study will shed more light on these reintegration obstacles, while evaluating an alcohol and drug abuse program designed to better offender's reintegration outcomes while reducing recidivism.

This moral panic, also well known as the *War on Drugs,* was an initiative first undertaken by the United States to wage an all out offensive (as President Nixon described it in 1971) against the use of certain illegal drugs. A 1989 Congressional Research Service report argued that the nation's war on drugs could have began as early as the development of public policy in November 1880 when the United States and China signed an agreement prohibiting the shipment of opium between the two countries (Central Intelligence Agency, 2007:92). This has fueled the expansion of the U.S. prison industry, which now oversees the largest prison population in the world, reaching a total of approximately two and one-quarter million inmates in 2006 (Sabol *et al.*, 2006).

The chapter will briefly synthesize the *incarceration binge* (Austin, 2001) in the United States today, with a particular focus on (i) recidivism in the United States and (ii) the drug-crime nexus. This study on Lake City adds to the significant works that explain the complexities surrounded in offender recidivism (coined the *Black Box* by Gendreau and Ross in 1979) within a systems approach to correctional reentry programming. This chapter provides the foundation for the development of future chapters by explaining the problems associated with correctional reentry in Lake City and the United States.

THE INCARCERATION BINGE

Offender and correctional reentry is not a universal or systematic concept. Decades of legislation such as zero tolerance and truth in sentencing have increased the number of persons incarcerated and hardened the conditions of confinement. Today, there are mounting concerns that the increasing number of people released from prison, nearly 650,000 people per year, could be posing significant public safety issues (Glaze and Bonczar, 2006:1) where 1600 people are being released from prisons across our communities each day.

A majority of people only need to locate an introduction to corrections textbook to understand that the origins and purposes of jails and prisons was to remove dangerous persons from their communities and place them into isolation for the greater good of the community. However, in this author's opinion, jails and prisons have now become the answer to all of our criminal misbehaviors. Rather than simply incarcerating those persons who are dangerous to others, we use the prison key as a means to deter all criminals, whether they are violent or not. This has inevitably led correctional agencies to give parole to dangerous offenders simply because of the overcrowding of drug and/or non-violent criminals. This poses immediate safety risks for all of us.

The number of people incarcerated under state and federal control has increased dramatically over the past eight decades (Hughes and Hickman, 2006). In 1925, there were 91,669 state and federal prisoners and the rate of incarceration was only 79 per 100,000 of the resident population. Based on growth projections, the United States has the highest incarceration rate in the world, incarcerating approximately 850,000 people in jails each day and 1.6 to 1.7 million in prisons across the country.

This combination means that nearly 2.5 million people across the United States are behind bars. This equates to approximately 775 people for every 100,000 (Walmsley, 2006:1). This translates into approximately one adult for every 100 (PEW, 2008).

This change in the correctional landscape is likely due to the shift in a sentencing philosophy from rehabilitation to deterrence and/or incapacitation. The change in correctional philosophy seems to have grown out of frustration with offenders who refuse to change, the failure of rehabilitative programs to reduce recidivism, and the need to punish offenders (Petersilia, 2004b). The human costs notwithstanding, it seems clear that taxpayers cannot sustain this trend, let alone permit it to accelerate (National Association of State Budget Officers [NASBO], 2004).

Nearly everyone, approximately 98%, of people admitted to correctional facilities will return to the community at some point (Petersilia, 2004a; Sabol *et al.*, 2007). This will inevitably result in a corresponding explosion of jail and prison releases. In addition to the dramatic increase in the number of prisoners, another historical trend has significantly reshaped the context in which reentry occurs in the United States. Research has identified that prisoners are increasingly completing their sentence in and out of correctional institutions. A significant majority (more than four of every five) of returning offenders were subjected to some period of post-prison supervision in the community before being released (Hughes *et al.*, 2001). Therefore, one in five, or 20% of offenders have no supervision in their communities. This thwarts the public perception that offenders are incarcerated for their entire sentence (via judge or jury). The release of offenders on parole, often before completing their prison terms has resulted in significant safety risks often voiced by both criminal justice practitioners and citizens alike (Hughes *et al.*, 2001).

As jail and prison populations swell, so do correctional budgets. American taxpayers spent $9 billion for corrections in 1982. According to the National Association of State Budget Officers (2008), with the possible exception of health care spending, spending on corrections over the past 20 years has increased more than any other major spending category (other than military expenditures). In 1987, all states collectively spent $10.6 billion, as well as their primary pool of discretionary tax dollars on corrections. By 2008, states spent more than $49 billion, a 315% increase in twenty years. Based on data collected from the National Association of State Budget Officers (2008), (adjusted to 2007 dollars), the increase was 127%. Inevitably, tax payers are choosing incarceration over other social priorities such as health care, education and social security (to only name a few).

In 2008 alone, the total state spending on corrections, which included bonds and federal contributions increased to $49 billion, rising from only $12 billion in 1987. By 2011, continued prison growth is expected to cost states almost $75 billion (Public Safety, 2008:2). As prison populations grow, so does the average per prisoner operating cost which varies widely by state, but based on recent statistics, the average cost was $23,876 in 2005 (PEW, 2007:ii). The state of Rhode Island spent the most per inmate ($44,860) while Louisiana had the lowest per inmate cost (Public Safety, 2007:iii). Not surprisingly, 13 states now devote more than $1 billion a year to fund their correctional systems. California spent $8.8 billion in 2008, which is a 216% increase from 20 years ago. For Californians, this is only expected to increase further as Governor Schwarzenegger authorized an additional $7.9 billion in capital spending for 53,000 prison and jail beds (PEW, 2007: ii).

Legislators agree that there simply will not be enough money in state budgets to continue to support these budget increases. This *incarceration binge* (Austin, 2001:1) has become a political reality which is now affecting economic choices and communities as a whole. While this legislative and political moral panic toughens legislation against drug users, it perpetuates the belief that get tough strategies are effective. However, as explained previously, these get tough sentences are indirectly allowing offenders to be released early (via parole) to make way for new criminals in the prison systems. This indirectly creates public safety risks and ultimately continues to overwhelm an already overpopulated criminal justice correctional system.

Despite this perceived budgetary investment in the criminal justice correctional system, the likelihood of a former prisoner succeeding in the community upon his or her release has not improved. To inevitably try to reduce spending on corrections, some policymakers have managed the growth of inmate and jail populations using truth in sentencing laws with probation and parole. Therefore, violators of probation and parole represent the fastest growing category of admissions to corrections facilities (Blumstein and Beck, 1999). This is creating a churning effect of offenders reintegrating into jails and prisons. Other options available to state and local government officials simply do not generate any meaningful savings.

The number of correctional officers and staff cannot be reduced, unless there can be an assumption of corresponding declines in the inmate population. This option jeopardizes the safety of staff, inmates, and of course, the community itself. Cuts to the quality or availability of services also present few opportunities for savings. However, that is exactly what is occurring.

Resources to reduce the obstacles and barriers that offenders face when reentering their communities are being cut and/or eliminated. Many state correctional departments report being under some form of federal court supervision because of over-crowding or the insufficiency of services available to inmates. Practically every state is facing at least the threat of litigation. Correctional administrators find themselves cutting programs and/or services (rather than personnel) which likely lessens the likelihood of successful offender reintegration. A majority of wardens have fewer resources and perhaps a lessened interest in the services and supports offenders will need upon their release from prison and jail. Simply put, correctional and criminal justice budgets are in crises, and as a result, many institutions are reducing the quality and quantity of services and supports offenders need to reintegrate into their communities. Tough on crime, zero tolerance laws, mandatory minimum statutes, three strikes and you're out sentencing, and truth in sentencing statutes have not only increased the prison population in the United States, but also increased the cyclical recidivism rate of offenders who are unable to change their lifestyle to better reintegrate into their communities.

Many people consider correctional reentry and incarceration simply to be a social problem. There is a feeling among some people that if someone commits a crime that they should be punished, and prisons should be that punitive environment. Often, these people have not been to or know someone who has survived the prison environment. It is for this reason that the author chose to explain offender reintegration as a political problem (that has economic and social consequences). As correctional budgets continue to rise, each taxpayer should be concerned with the rising numbers of those incarcerated and ex-offenders who are churning or cycling through the criminal justice system.

Recidivism

There are several measurements being employed to measure offender recidivism. Research by prominent scholars have argued that recidivism can be measured using probation and parole violations, absconding from the criminal justice system, re-arrest for a new crime, re-conviction, and re-incarceration (Taxman and Cherkos, 1995; Petersilia, 1999). Estimates of recidivism will often vary with the length of the follow up period and the different measurements selected. Re-arrest refers to any arrest for a felony or serious misdemeanor charge. Re-conviction refers to the conviction of at least one charge after the date of release from prison. Re-incarceration refers to either an offender's return to prison or any new admission to a local jail or prison with a sentence for a new offense.

After comparing the 1983 and 1994 national studies on recidivism, Langan and Levin (2002:8) note that only offender re-arrest rates had risen. The overall re-arrest rate rose sharply between 1983 and 1994. In 1983, 62.5% were re-arrested within three years and of the 272,111 released in 1994, re-arrest increased to 67.5%. This re-arrest statistic held definitively for all released offenders. Property offenders arrest rates increased from 68% to 74% respectively (Langan and Levin, 2002:6). Released violent offenders recidivism rates had a relatively small increase of 60% to 62% between 1983 and 1994 (Langan and Levin, 2002:8). Released drug offenders increased from 50% to 67% respectively. Released public order offender recidivism rates for arrest also increased from 55% to 62%.

Between 1983 and 1994, the overall offender re-conviction rate did not increase significantly, remaining at approximately 47% (Langan and Levin, 2002:8). Similarly, there were no significant changes for released property, violent or public order offenders. The only significant change in re-conviction rates between 1983 and 1994 was for drug offenders. Among drug offenders released in 1983, 35% were re-convicted for a new crime (not necessarily another drug offense). These statistics identify a trend of targeting drug offenders. Among those released in 1994, the re-conviction percentage was significantly higher at 47% (Langan and Levin, 2002:8).

Over one-quarter of offenders released in 1994 had returned to either a state or federal prison as a result of another prison sentence (due to violating their probation/ parole or a new criminal activity). This does not include offenders that were sentenced to jail time. Of the quarter of offenders re-incarcerated, over half (52%) of offenders were re-incarcerated because they had violated a technical condition of their release, such as failing a drug test, missing an appointment with their parole officer. Approximately 48% of offenders were re-incarcerated because they had committed a new misdemeanor or felony crime (Langan and Levin, 2002:4-6).

With more offenders being released from jail and/or prison than any time before in American history, practitioners and academics continue to generate working hypotheses and studies to determine what is, and what is not working in correctional reentry programming to reduce recidivism rates.

The inescapable conclusion is that Americans have paid a price for the offender recidivism and churning which has contributed to this *incarceration binge* (Austin, 2001:1). Offenders continue to leave prison and return to their communities with less treatment, fewer skills, less exposure to the world of work, and less focused attention on planning for a smooth transition.

Although much has been written on probation and parole recidivism, there has been considerably less written on the specific violations of probationers/parolees while under community supervision. Studies of probation most often report the failure rates of probationers. Therefore, comparatively little was reported about the specific behaviors (or vents) that have led to an offender's failure of probation (Petersilia, 2001). Studies devoted to the incidences of probation violations, including new crimes that occur while a probationer serves his or her sentence, were equally scarce. The current study attempts to bridge this gap in the literature by providing more detail on the process of reintegration.

Offenders under community supervision for probation and/or parole accounted for a majority, approximately 70% of all offenders within the criminal justice system in 2004 (down from approximately 74% in 1990), while those incarcerated accounted for 30% (up from 26% in 1990) (Glaze and Bonczar, 2006:4). At least 95% of all state prisoners will be released from prison at some point and nearly 80% will be released to parole supervision (Glaze and Bonczar, 2006:4). The rate of probation and parole violations also increased significantly over recent years. According to the Bureau of Justice Statistics, the successful completion rate of probation has dropped from 74% in 1986 to 60% in 1990 (Glaze, 2001:3). Taxman and Cherkos (1995) have attributed this drop to more stringent conditions of probation and/or parole orders that increase the likelihood for violations. In 1985, nearly 70% of parolees successfully completed their parole term and by 1997, that number had dropped to 44% (Glaze, 2003:7).

Conversely, the percentage of those offenders who fail on parole has increased from less than a third of all parolees in 1985 to 54% in 1997 (Petersilia, 1999: 212). Almost 9% of all parolees nationally were identified as absconding, meaning their whereabouts were unknown to their parole agents (Bonczar and Glaze, 1999:7).

Based on financial and budgetary constraints, states are having difficulty assisting these offenders reintegrating back into their communities, which subsequently has a churning effect through the criminal justice system. Petersilia (2004a) argues that offender reentry may be simply defined as all activities and programming conducted to prepare ex-convicts to return safely to the community and live as law abiding citizens. Petersilia argues that this includes various processes from the duration of incarceration and how each offender spends their time during confinement to the process by which an offender is released, and how each offender is further supervised after release. Based on this philosophy, it can be argued that successful offender reentry can only be accomplished through a relationship between an offender's reentry plan for programming and reintegration.

As Gendreau and Ross (1979) suggest, recidivism may be more complex than simply measuring arrest, conviction and incarceration rates. Gendreau and Ross argue that researchers and practitioners must look further into the complexities of recidivism and determine which programs and services would be the most successful in reducing recidivism. This coined term, the *Black Box,* was the launching pad for this study in that the author wanted to identify whether Lake City's *ATR* program was effective in curbing alcohol and drug abuse and/or recidivism.

DRUG-CRIME NEXUS

According to the Office of National Drug Control Policy, the United States spends approximately $600.00 per second on drug suppression (Drug Sense, 2010). American public policy seems to be clear: arrest and incarcerate drug criminals. This drug-crime nexus results in a person arrested every seventeen seconds for a drug offense (based on 2007 Federal Bureau of Investigation Uniform Crime Reports). A popular U.S. Department of Justice statistics website estimates that the war on drugs cost taxpayers over $50 billion per year and that with each arrest, another person will be incarcerated for a drug offense for every hour of every day in 2010 (Drug Sense, 2010).

As explained previously, the United States has been waging a *War on Drugs* since it was first initiated by President Nixon in 1971. Almost forty years later, legislators and crime control advocates have concluded that the war on drugs has not been effective and may never be won. According to the Central Intelligence Agency (CIA), hundreds of billions of tax dollars have been spent on this war, yet legislators and crime control advocates were nowhere near winning it (World Factbook, 2007). Drug use and abuse still continues today almost unabated. Heroin, cocaine, methamphetamine and other illicit drugs are cheaper, purer, and easier to get than ever before. In 2004, over one million people were behind bars on drug charges alone (Petersilia, 2004a:4).

To appreciate the gravity of this number, consider that the number of people behind bars in the United States for drug offenses was greater than the number of people who were incarcerated in all of Western Europe for all criminal offenses (Walmsley, 2006). It should also be noted that Western Europe has a larger population than the 307 million people currently living in the United States. Perhaps most troubling within American drug policy is the continued over representation of minorities within the American correctional system (Tonry, 1987). The war on drugs, despite its intent, has become a war on families, a war on public health, and a war on American's constitutional rights. There may, perhaps, be no other public policy in the United States which still continues to be funded at exponential levels despite a track record of failures (Walker *et al.*, 2008).

The infamous Robert Martinson's article arguing "what works" in correctional treatment and programming (1974) scholarship led scholars from different disciplines to dispute Martinson's findings that nothing works and subsequently, have generated data on the effectiveness of offender rehabilitation programs (Gendreau and Ross, 1979; Cullen and Gendreau, 2000; Andrews and Bonta, 1998; Sherman *et al.*, 1997;

MacKenzie and Hickman, 1998). These studies suggest that several community programs have been found to be effective in reducing offender recidivism. More recent scholarly findings suggest that intensive community programs (at least six months long), a focus on high risk offenders (based on standardized instrumentation), which use cognitive-behavioral treatment techniques, and a matched therapist and program to the specific learning styles and characteristics of individual offenders have been found to be the most effective (Sherman *et al.*, 1997; Aos *et al.*, 2006).

Sherman's (1999) evidence based policing paradigm proposed that decision making should be based on the strength of the evidence. Associating this paradigm to corrections would argue that evidence based decision making should use research to guide practice and evaluate programs. The goal would be to use scientific evidence to hold officials, practitioners and researchers accountable for their practices. Sherman would argue that academics and practitioners should focus and concentrate their efforts on determining what does work and make commitments to increasing program efficacy. Thus, this systems approach is what will be explored in an effort to understanding the black box of reentry from an offender's alcohol and other drug abuse to their potential recidivism. The Lake City *Access To Recovery* (*ATR*) program proposes the use of scientific outcome based principles and factors within the literature to derive offender success: a systems based, holistic, client-driven re-integrative approach of rehabilitation for offenders returning from prison.

LAKE CITY ACCESS TO RECOVERY (ATR)

President George W. Bush announced a new substance abuse treatment initiative in his 2004 State of the Union Address, formally known as *Access To Recovery* (*ATR*). This new initiative would provide people seeking drug and alcohol treatment with vouchers to pay for a range of appropriate community based services. Congress appropriated nearly $600 million between 2004 and 2007 from the Substance Abuse and Mental Health

Services Administration (SAMHSA) to launch the initiative (2006). After a competitive grant process that reviewed applications from 44 states and 22 tribes and territories, funds were awarded to 14 states and one tribal organization: California, Connecticut, Florida, Idaho, Illinois, Louisiana, Missouri, New Jersey, New Mexico, Tennessee, Texas, Washington, Wisconsin, Wyoming, and the California Rural Indian Health Board, to implement *ATR* (SAMHSA, 2006). Lake City's jurisdiction received approximately $30 million in funding over a three year period.

The Lake City *ATR* program identifies alcohol and other drug abuse (AODA) treatment as the primary priority of the grant. The expectation of the grant voucher program was to provide AODA programming to those populations most at risk of illegal drug use. Based on the drug--crime nexus assumption, there was a secondary expectation that addiction treatment could reduce criminal activity by 80% (Substance Abuse and Mental Health Services Administration, 2006). Therefore, a significant aspect of this voucher based grant program would allow for offenders released from prison and jail to receive AODA treatment and resource assistance which could further reduce their likelihood of recidivism. Resource allocation towards alcohol and other drug use in itself has already shown increases in employment opportunities and decreased homelessness, which could result in substantially improved physical and mental health (SAMHSA, 2006).

Each federally funded *ATR* program was expected to establish a grantee voucher program for substance abuse clinical treatment and recovery support services premised on three principles (SAMSHA, 2006). First, because the process of recovery is a personal one, offender (client) choice becomes an integral aspect of the *ATR* programming. Achieving alcohol and other drug abuse recovery can take various pathways: physical, mental, emotional, and/or spiritual (Lake City proposal, 2003). By receiving a grantee voucher, offenders in need of addiction treatment and resource support would be able to choose the providers that they felt could assist them. This increased choice, according to the Lake City grant would also increase and encourage quality practices. Second, the grant proposed using outcome-based success measurements such as abstinence from AODA, stable housing, access to resources, attainment of employment, enrollment in school and a lessened involvement with the criminal justice system. This program was expected to expand both clinical treatment and recovery support services while also expanding the array of services available, which could include medical detoxification, inpatient and outpatient treatment modalities, residential services, peer support, relapse prevention, case management, and other recovery support services (SAMHSA, 2006). This would formally allow religious based agencies access to these treatment and recovery support services. As a result, this three-prong purpose would increase the capacity of agencies able to assist offenders at risk for alcohol and drug abuse and perhaps reduce the burden placed on the criminal justice system in Lake City.

Within Lake City (the jurisdiction under examination), the state's Department of Corrections had established an alternative to incarceration program. This allowed the state's Department of Corrections to collaborate directly with Lake City's *ATR* administrators to accept all probationers and parolees who reported and volunteered for the AODA treatment program (Lake City, 2003).

Offenders of the Lake City *ATR* program seeking drug and alcohol treatment and recovery support were assessed by qualified clinical staff and received a voucher to pay for a range of appropriate services. Within Lake City, the grantee agencies were expected to work with a consortium of public and private entities to jointly administer the program, distribute vouchers, and deliver alcohol and drug treatment and other ancillary services (Lake City, 2003). This consortium would be required to monitor offender outcomes and make adjustments based on the cost effectiveness of the services received. The key to accountability of this new treatment initiative would be in the linking of reimbursement for services to a demonstrated abstinence from drug and alcohol use by offenders following discharge. This study outlines two research models to explore the effectiveness of the Lake City ATR program and whether the program reduced offender recidivism.

RESEARCH MODEL I

The first research model explored the effectiveness of the Lake City *ATR* program. Two dependent variables were used to determine effectiveness. The first dependent variable measured whether each participant abstained from any alcohol and/or other drug usage. This could become a crucial factor in determining whether an offender would be successful at the onset of their release into the community. The second dependent variable used to gauge the effectiveness of the *ATR* program was whether the offender was successful in their completion of their client chosen treatment program (which could have lasted from one day to fourteen months).

This model sought to explain the significant complexities and variability within the successes and failures of correctional programming. Scholars argue that there are many outcomes that reentry programs strive to improve upon, and that these are rarely measured in traditional recidivism outcome evaluations (Petersilia, 2004b; Visher *et al.*, 2004). In an effort to explain this black box of reintegration, the author was interested in examining several factors known to increase or decrease an offender's success in reducing their AODA and/or recidivism: AODA treatment modalities, faith based treatment, and barriers to offender reintegration.

RESEARCH MODEL II

The second research model would determine whether Lake City's *ATR* program was effective in reducing offender recidivism during an offender's treatment programming. The researcher conceptualized recidivism using five measurements: (i) one or more documented incidences of technical probation or parole violations; (ii) a warrant for non-compliance of an offender's terms of probation/parole (which could include absconding from custody); (iii) arrest for a charge of a new crime; (iv) conviction of a new crime; and/or (v) incarceration of an offender.

CHAPTER 2:

Examining the Process of Reentry

This chapter explains the factors associated with the successes and failures of offender reentry in the United States. Due to the current prison explosion or *incarceration binge* (Austin, 2001:1) within the United States, offenders face significant barriers when re-entering into their communities. Based on empirical research, this chapter will synthesize the drug-crime nexus, barriers and improvements in offender resources, recidivism, and how a system based approach has improved the process of offender reintegration. These motivating factors represent the bulk of what we know about correctional offender re-entry, focusing particularly on the major factors associated with the current study's *Access To Recovery* (*ATR*) alcohol and other drug use treatment program.

Virtually every person incarcerated in a jail and nearly 98% of those incarcerated in prisons will eventually be released (Petersilia, 2004a). According to the most recent estimates, approximately 650,000 people were released from prison in 2004, while over seven million different individuals were released from jails across the United States (Hammett, 2000:20). While both figures were historically high, they will certainly be eclipsed by the number of people released from corrections facilities this decade if incarceration rates persist (Harrison and Karberg, 2004). With over two million people currently incarcerated, and over twelve million people with prior felony convictions, the criminal justice system faces tremendous challenges in reintegrating this large and growing population of people to their communities, where they reside (Pager, 2003).

The per capita rate of imprisonment in America hovered at about 110 per 100,000 from 1925 to 1973, with little variation (Blumstein and Beck, 1999:17). However, the per capita incarceration rate began increasing in 1973 and has grown steadily to its current 2007 levels of 755 persons per 100,000, almost seven times the 1973 level (Walmsley, 2006). Local, state and federal jails and prisons now house over two million people, a threefold increase since 1980 (Glaze and Bonczar, 2006:2).

The number of prisoners under state and federal jurisdictions has increased dramatically over the past eight decades. In 1925, there were 91,669 state and federal prisoners and the rate of incarceration was only 79 per 100,000 of the resident population. By the end of 2000, the number of incarcerated offenders rose to 1,321,137, which translates into a rate of incarceration of 478 per 100,000 residents.

At midyear 2004, Bureau of Justice Statisticians Harrison and Beck (2004:1) reported that the Nation's prisons and jails incarcerated 2,131,180 persons. Prisoners in the custody of the 50 states and the federal system accounted for two-thirds of the incarcerated population (1,410,404 inmates). The other third were held in local jails (713,990), not including persons in community based programs. In June of 2004, 1,494,216 prisoners were under state and federal jurisdiction. This includes inmates in custody and persons under the legal jurisdiction of a prison system but held outside its facilities (Harrison and Beck, 2004:2). At midyear 2004, local jail facilities held or supervised 84,538 offenders. Almost ten percent of these offenders (70,548) were supervised outside jail facilities in programs such as community service, work release, weekend reporting, electronic monitoring, and other alternative programs (Harrison and Beck, 2004:7).

Based on projections of correctional growth, the United States has the highest incarceration rate in the world, incarcerating approximately 850,000 people in jails each day and 1.6 to 1.7 million in prisons across the country. This combination means that nearly 2.5 million people across the United States are behind bars. This equates to approximately 775 people for every

100,000 (Walmsley, 2006:1) or one adult for every 100 (PEW, 2008). As of 2007 Bureau of Justice Statistics, 1,596,127 people were in state or federal prison custody, and another 723,131 were in local jails. This adult inmate count at the beginning of 2007 was 2,319,258 (Sabol, 2006). Based on the 2010 United States Census Bureau estimates, the number of adults in the United States was approximately 230 million (for 2008). This inevitably means that the actual incarceration rate was 1 in every 99.1 adults (PEW, 2008:6).

These aggregate incarceration statistics often mask significantly higher incarceration rates for particular demographic groups. Mid-year 2006 data from the U.S. Department of Justice shows that black and Hispanic men were disproportionately more likely to be incarcerated within their lifetime than someone who identifies as a white male. When factoring in age, one in every 15 black males aged 18 or older was in prison or jail, while black men over 55 had a rate of one in 115 (Sabol, 2007). These disparities continue to plague the correctional system and ultimately have political, economic and societal effects in all jurisdictions, not just Lake City.

The total local, state, and federal adult correctional population incarcerated or in the community has increased to over seven million people. Data was collected annually through the use of the Bureau of Justice Statistics, Annual Probation Survey and the Annual Parole Survey. Their findings indicate that about 3.2% of the U.S. adult population, or 1 in every 32 adults, were incarcerated and/or on probation or parole in 2005 (Glaze and Bonczar, 2006:1). The probation population in 2005 reached new levels. At last count, 4,162,536 were on probation in the United States. The adult parole population reached a total of 784,408 at yearend 2005 (Glaze and Bonczar, 2006:1). With an exploding incarceration rate, there is evidence that practitioners and researchers need to explore the black box of correctional reentry to make sense of offender recidivism.

The Black Box: Beyond Recidivism

> *Reentry is the inevitable consequence of incarceration. With the exception of those who die of natural consequences or are executed [in prison], everyone placed in confinement is eventually released. Reentry is not an option.*
>
> *(Travis and Visher, 2005:78)*

As explained by Travis and Visher, an offender's reintegration into their community is not an option but rather a process within one's lifetime. Below are barriers that offenders may face on a daily basis that we may or may not have encountered in our lives and/or taken for granted. Each of these programs are usually considered symbolic or buzzword components of any department of corrections' model of offender reintegration. Perhaps the most crucial components within any approach to reintegration are whether local municipalities and programs have the necessary resources to adequately address offender's treatment and/or recovery.

Drug-Crime Nexus

Perhaps the most essential aftercare is the availability of alcohol and drug abuse (AODA) programming for offenders released from prison. National surveys suggest that approximately 80% of state prisoners and 70% of federal prisoners had self reported past alcohol and drug abuse (Mumbo, 1999:14). Mumbo also reports that nearly one-fifth (16%) of offenders reported having committed their current crime to obtain funds for illicit drugs. Why would we expect that inmates, once released would not return to this lifestyle? While there may be AODA programs available for offenders during their time in prison, there is no simulation that can portray the realities of what offenders will face when challenged with the freedom to use alcohol and/or drugs.

The drug-crime nexus; the connection between the abuse of illegal drugs and crime has been well documented (Goldstein,

1985; Tonry and Wilson, 1990). While most correctional administrators recognize that most offenders are substance abusers, there is a void in the time period in which an offender is released from prison and when they may be able to enter treatment. This is likely due to waitlists or the lack of department resources.

Release is certainly considered a stressful time for an offender, making it even more difficult for him/her to avoid a relapse to any alcohol or drug abuse. An offender's propensity to return to drinking and using drugs has a direct correlation with criminal activity (Tonry and Wilson, 1990). Therefore, many scholars and practitioners have argued that it is critical that offenders who leave prison must have immediate access to programs for a continuity of care to assist in both reducing the likelihood of AODA abuse and criminal recidivism. Today, the percentage of people released from prison following a conviction for a drug offense is 20% higher than it was in 1984, totaling about one-third of all released prisoners (Hughes *et al.*, 2001:73). Between 1980 and 2003, the number of inmates in the United States has also quadrupled thereby adding more strain to an already overburdened and overpopulated criminal justice system. This has been particularly damaging to state prison populations which have increased more than 300% to approximately 1.25 million people over the last twenty five years (Harrison and Beck, 2004:1).

These increases have been fueled mainly by drug related crime as well as more arrests, convictions, and lengthier sentences for drug crimes (Belenko, 2000). Offenders who regularly used drugs or alcohol while incarcerated have been found to have higher recidivism rates than other offenders. National offending studies have found that within three years of an offender's release, approximately 95% of state offenders with drug use histories would return to regular drug use (Leshner, 1998). Of those offenders who returned to regular drug use over 68% were re-arrested, 47% were re-convicted, and 25% were sentenced to prison for a new crime (Langan and Levin, 2002:91).

The high rates of drug involvement and recidivism among arrestees and inmates raise even more challenges for supervising offenders following release. At the end of 2003, there were 4,848,575 offenders under community supervision (including 4,073,987 on probation and 774,588 on parole), more than twice the number of inmates in correctional facilities (Glaze and Palla, 2004:1-2). Nearly two-thirds of offenders had a history of illegal drug use, including 31% who used cocaine or crack (Mumola, 1999:6). More than 630,000 prison inmates were released to the community in 2002 after completing their sentences or being released to parole supervision (Harrison and Karberg, 2004:11) and 80% were released to parole. Take into account that rates of technical violations of parole conditions were also high (Beck and Mumola, 1999). In 1998, 37% of state prison commitments were for violations of parole or other conditional release (Langan and Levin, 2002). Therefore, the repeated recycling or churning of offenders into jails and/or prisons have devastating consequences on both informal (families and personal relationships) and formal support systems (Clear *et al.*, 2001). Clearly, this had an effect on an offender's reintegration into their community, including having the ability to create reliable ties with new support networks (Clear *et al.,* 2001) while addressing any pressing health and social needs (Travis *et al.,* 2001).

In 1998, The Arrestee Drug Abuse Monitoring (ADAM) study found that nearly 80% of offenders reported past drug and/or alcohol use. Another 51% to 79% of the arrestees (with a median of 65%) had positive urinalysis at the time of the arrest for marijuana, cocaine/crack, heroin and opiates, methamphetamines, phencyclidine (PCP), and benzodiazepines (National Institute of Justice, 2000). Using the DSM IV (Diagnostic and Statistical Manual of Mental Disorders, 4th Edition) criteria to define drug dependency, over 38% of offenders were found to have been AODA dependent and in need of treatment (Zhang, 2004:85). Based on these studies and further study on alcohol and drug abuse, approximately half of offenders were considered heavy drug users based on the commonly accepted criteria of using drugs for at least 13 days per month (National Institute of Justice, 2000).

Further evaluation of Arrestee Drug Abuse Monitoring (ADAM) program data indicates that a range of 42% to 86% of adult male arrestees (in 39 sites) and 52% to 82% of female arrestees (in 25 sites) tested positive for marijuana, cocaine, opiates, methamphetamine, or phencyclidine (Zhang, 2004:85). Between one-quarter and one-half of male arrestees, and one-third to two-thirds of female arrestees were reported to be at risk for drug dependence. Over two-thirds of state prison inmates reported regular lifetime illicit drug use (Belenko, 2002:15). Four in every ten state prison inmates reported having used cocaine, 27% reported crack usage, and 21% heroin usage. More than 80% of state prison inmates had indications of a serious drug or alcohol involvement (Belenko and Peugh, 2005:38).

Nearly 80% of offenders within the state prison population reported a history of drug and/or alcohol use, of which 74% were due to be released (Beck, 2000; Mumola, 1999). Only 10% of those offenders in state prison and 3% of offenders in local jails received formal treatment prior to their release (Mumola, 1999:19). Despite a significant infusion of federal monies to fund treatment in state prisons, only 10% of state inmates reported participating in professional substance abuse treatment, a reduction of 25% since 1991 (Beck, 2000). Approximately one-quarter (24%) of state offenders had participation in some drug abuse programs (i.e. self help groups or educational programs) in 1997. This was a reduction from 30% of participants in 1991 (Beck, 2000). Of the soon to be released group (using drugs in the month prior to incarceration), 18% participated in treatment since prison admission while 22% of alcohol abusers participated (Beck, 2000:5). Therefore, the high rates of substance abuse and relapse and the difficulty of accessing effective treatment (both while in custody and in the community) greatly complicated reintegration. This failure to address the post release and continuity of care for offenders with substance abuse will have a direct effect on their success while on probation/parole and likelihood of criminal activity (Taxman *et al.,* 2002).

The concern about the connections between criminal justice policy and drug treatment policy was brought into focus by two distinct research findings made by Harrison (2001). Harrison argues that the continuity of care (or the in-prison drug treatment in the period leading up to release) can, if combined with treatment in the post release period, significantly reduce both drug use and recidivism. Therefore, any additional planning of treatment programs along with supervision during reentry can enhance the health and safety of offenders. Harrison also concludes that this "addiction is a brain disease" (Leshner, 1998:2; Harrison, 2001). Consequently, the return of a former addict to their old neighborhood places that offender at high risk of relapse, in part because the offender's old habits and experience act as a trigger to the brain to heighten the cravings of drugs. Therefore, the idea of criminal justice policy requiring an offender to return to their community may be complicating the offender's potential risk factors of relapse. Without intervention, inmates who return to their communities will invariably repeat the same types of behaviors that led to their incarceration. This was further exemplified in statistics showing that in 1997, 46% of state inmates and 26% of federal inmates were on probation or parole when they were incarcerated (General Accounting Office, 2000:3). Addressing the treatment needs of drug involved offenders should be of critical importance in reducing the costs of the crime, including re-incarceration, other criminal justice costs, and social costs.

There is significant evidence that offender rehabilitation programs that target alcohol and other drug abuse can be effective (Andrews and Bonta, 1998; Gendreau *et al.,* 1995; Aos *et al.*, 2006). Meta-analyses support that if programs are structured and used multiple treatment components, offenders will be more likely to abstain from using drugs (in the short term). Using behavioral and cognitive methods for directed skills would be more effective than nondirective counseling focusing on insight, self-esteem, or disclosure. Meaningful contact between the counselor and offender could also be effective in addressing the characteristics associated with an offender's criminal history.

Several studies have explored the relationship between drug using and criminal behavior to determine the offender's criminal and drug using career (Nurco *et al.*, 1981; Lipton *et al.*, 2000; Inciardi *et al.*, 2004). Research indicates that chronic users of heroin, cocaine, and crack commit a vast amount of crime. In extensive longitudinal studies of addict careers in Baltimore, Nurco *et al.* (1981) found there were higher rates of criminality among heroin users during periods of addiction than during periods of non-addiction. Lipton and Johnson interviewed hundreds of criminally active drug users recruited from the streets of east and central Harlem. Their study documented the wide range of heroin usage rates among addicts and the clear correlation between the usage of heroin and incidence of crime committed (Lipton *et al.*, 2000). Studies conducted in Miami, Florida, demonstrated the vast amount of crime was committed by crack users (Inciardi *et al., 2004*).

Altogether, these findings can imply that the use of heroin, cocaine, and other drugs may not necessarily initiate a criminal career but it can intensify and perpetuate a career. Incarceration obviously halts these crimes against society acting as both a deterrent and withdrawal for most drug abusers. However, research shows that when those who were addicted to drugs before they were incarcerated return to their communities and resume their addicted and criminal lifestyle (Inciardi *et al.*, 1997). Considering the costs to society, it would be prudent to develop resources for ex-offenders and their communities.

As outlined in the prison based treatment literature, cognitive and behavioral interventions should be offered during the last six to nine months of an offender's incarceration and emphasize both recovery goals and the offender's transition to continuing treatment in the community (Prendergast *et al.,* 1999). Ample evidence suggests that the continuity of in-prison therapeutic groups with the completion of aftercare treatment (which is cognitive based) is effective in reducing recidivism (Knight et al., 2002; Martin et al., 1999; Dowden et al., 2003; Inciardi et al., 2004).

Knight *et al.* studied the effectiveness of intensive treatment when integrated with alcohol and drug abuse aftercare. Their first study in 1997 indicated that 80% of the 222 offenders who took part in the therapeutic community programming graduated and as such, had lower levels of AODA use and criminal behavior after six months of release (Knight *et al.*, 2002). Those who completed the first phase of their aftercare program had lower relapse and recidivism rates than did the parolees in the comparison sample. In 1999, Knight *et al.* completed a three year follow-up study, based on the 291 follow-up eligible parolees. This study found that offenders who completed the program and aftercare were the least likely to be re-incarcerated (25%), compared to 64% of aftercare dropouts and 42% of untreated comparison groups (Knight *et al.*, 2002).

Martin *et al.* (1999) examined the success of therapeutic communities, finding that program effects declined over a three year period after release. Their Maryland study also found that the effects remained significant when program participation, completion, and aftercare were taken into account. Offenders in AODA programming who completed secondary community treatment were found to do better than offenders with no treatment, and those offenders who dropped out of the programming. Offenders who received post-prison aftercare in the community were more likely to be abstinent and less likely to be re-arrested for a new crime. The researchers suggested that post-release AODA treatment was the most effective when offenders continue their treatment for the purposes of long term success rather than simply short term assistance (Martin *et al.*, 1999). However, the initial concern in the process of intake is that offenders receive an assessment by a trained clinician to match each offender's needs with resources and services.

Assessment and Referral

The emphasis of this particular systems approach in Lake City is predicated on the initial assessment of the motivation and readiness for change, the severity of substance abuse and criminality problem, and special needs (e.g. clothing, housing, health, etc.) of each offender. Therefore, the outcomes of the assessment would be an appropriate placement (level of care) for each offender. The assessment process has multiple layers that are primarily focused on using clinical and psycho-social information to guide placement into the appropriate services. As discussed by McLellan and Woody (1998), matching clients to services can significantly improve outcomes. These outcomes can include: an offender's criminal justice history, history of substance abuse, mental health, family and social relationships, medical, education and employment. Therefore, utilizing an integrated systems process, Lake City utilized a variety of assessment tools to match an offender's needs with a consortium of public and private resources.

One prominent assessment tool that has been found to be effective in the assessment and evaluation of substance abuse was the Addiction Severity Index (ASI). It has been established as the standard assessment tool for alcohol and other addictions (Leonhard *et al.,* 2000). The ASI is an interview that assesses history, frequency, and consequences of alcohol and drug use, as well as five additional domains that are commonly associated with drug use: medical, legal, employment, social/family, and psychological functioning (McGahan *et al.*, 1986). Each offender receives an aggregate score of four for each of the five domains. A score of: no problem at all (0), slight problem (1), moderate problem (2), considerable problem (3), and extreme problem (4) which is further aggregated into a larger scaled total index to assist in a level of care assessment. The higher the score on the ASI indicates a greater need for treatment in each of these areas. These ASI scores can be used to profile patients' problem areas and then plan effective treatment (McGahan *et al.*, 1986).

Mäkelä's (2004) evaluation of 37 studies utilizing the ASI indicates high internal consistencies for three of the seven composite scores. Although the instrument does not produce consistent results in all studies, McLellan *et al.* (1982) suggested that the ASI should be considered a valid assessment tool. The researchers point out that three studies which would have strengthened the results were not included in Mäkelä's review of the literature.

A second instrument that was used as an assessment tool for offender alcohol and drug abuse is a clinically respected tool for patient placement; the American Society of Addiction Medicine Patient Placement Criteria or the ASAM – PPC 2nd Edition (Hoffmann *et al.,* 1991). The criteria used for admission, continued stay and discharge define four levels of care which can impact the (i) assessment of a patient's severity of illness; (ii) the treatment levels of care provided; and (iii) the clinical criteria that guide the most efficient placement of patients in the continuum of care. The ASAM provides an important resource to promote the flexible and cost effective treatment to conserve health care resources. The criteria allow clinicians, payers and policymakers to broaden the scope of available treatment options by placing greater emphasis on the continuum of care and encouraging flexible movement up or down the continuum (Hoffmann *et al.,* 2001).

The ASAM Patient Placement Criteria focuses on six dimensions to define an offender's potential level of care. These six dimensions include: (i) the potential for acute intoxication and/or withdrawal; (ii) biomedical conditions and complications; (iii) emotional/behavioral conditions or complications; (iv) treatment acceptance/resistance; (v) relapse potential; and (vi) recovery environment. Criteria listed under these six dimensions help guide placement to one of four levels of care, which is the first step in matching patients to treatment. Each of these defined levels of care would be essential to a further continuum of care: (i) hospitalized inpatient care; (ii) residential care; (iii) intensive outpatient care and (iv) outpatient care. The ASAM Patient Placement Criteria defined four roughly corresponding levels of care, but named them to be more descriptive of the intensity of services that should be provided to each offender (McGahan *et al.*, 1986). It is the intensity and duration of these programs that need to be explained to determine a person's level of care (with respect to programming).

Upon completing an offender's assessment (using the ASI and ASAM), it was the role of the Lake City clinical staff to locate a treatment provider that would provide each offender their adequate level of care (residential, inpatient and outpatient treatment). The purpose of allowing offenders to choose their program treatment provider was to increase an offender's motivation to change and improve their lives.

Rather than forcing an offender into a particular treatment program, choice could generate less resistance and higher program retention (Cullari, 1996). The willingness of offenders to participate in treatment while being supervised has been reported to be one of the most important aspects of successful implementation of a correctional reentry program (Astbury, 2008). Offenders are generally not given a choice about whether or not they wish to attend certain AODA programs and subsequently, they may feel they are participating involuntarily. While offenders may adhere to their probation/parole requirements, they may not be actively engaging. This *ATR* program is designed to ensure that, as Astbury suggests, offenders are not just occupying a seat and/or disrupting programming (Astbury, 2008:36). Lake City administrators expected that the combination of offender choice and the introduction of new treatment providers (that were able to provide faith based treatment) would increase AODA outcomes and decrease criminal activity.

Faith Based Treatment

Faith based programming has always been a complement to government welfare and criminal justice programs (McGarrell et al., 1999; Wuthnow, 2004). However, this form of programming has been criticized as jeopardizing the Church and State Establishment Clause in the United States Constitution. Thus, funding for such programs has been widely unpopular. Others who favor religious programming have argued that these religious organizations should not be unfairly excluded from a competition for government funding.

Based on the National Crime Policy Survey, Cullen *et al.* (2007) extracted 327 of 1000 respondents and assessed the public support for this Bush Administration's *Access To Recovery* policy initiative supporting funding for religious organizations. The study found that the respondents were evenly divided on the funding of the *ATR* programming. The study also found that a majority of respondents opposed having religious content within the AODA treatment programming. Further research suggested that other contentious issues were the hiring practices of organizations based on religious grounds and that funding should be equally given to all religious groups. The exploratory study also concluded that the respondents did not view faith based programming as a more or less effective correctional rehabilitation program.

With the development of Lake City's system based approach to offender reintegration, the program incorporated the offender and their informal support systems with their involvement with criminal justice practitioners. These informal support systems, such as family, friends and non-governmental organizations are the systems that will be in place long after their completion of treatment and/or probation/parole supervision. The most organized informal support networks that exist in abundance are churches.

Today, thousands of faith based organizations provide a range of services to individuals returning to their communities from prison. Churches can provide emergency shelter, housing, job training, mentoring, and treatment for addiction (Wilcox, 1998). These faith based providers give vital support for returning prisoners and the communities where they live. However, there is a lack of empirical research to support faith based programming is effective. Leaders of these churches and institutions are not necessarily trained, organized, or funded to support offenders returning from prison. In addition, there could be resentment (or division) within a congregation or members of the institution in whether to assist offenders who have a criminal background. Therefore, issues such as homelessness and health care assistance can be difficult to administer to assist offenders reentering into the community.

The literature review of faith based treatment and programming is still emerging. To date, the majority of literature indicates that religion influences various forms of delinquency, deviance and crime. The origins of the debate can be traced to social control theorists, Hirschi and Stark. Hirschi and Stark's (1969) research examined high school student religiosity as a factor of delinquency. Hirschi and Stark's failure to find significant effects of religiosity on crime resulted in a concerted effort by sociologists and criminologists to either refute or qualify this non-relationship. Also in 1969, Hirschi and Stack published Hellfire and Delinquency which questioned the link between hellfire and crime. The hellfire theory states that religion deters criminal behavior through the threat of supernatural sanctions and promotes normative behavior through the promise of supernatural rewards (1969:220). Hellfire theory measures the extent to which individuals who condemn an act on religiously based moral grounds are unlikely to contemplate engaging in delinquent behavior. This theory lays the foundation for religious tenets present in crime and punishment.

Religion has been empirically linked to restrain delinquent behavior; therefore, it should be logical to conclude that religion can assist in offender rehabilitation (Workman, 2005). The first penitentiaries in Europe and the United States were affiliated with religious institutions to assist in providing care and support for incarcerated and released prisoners. Religious teachings focus on promoting social values and morals, imparting offender accountability and responsibility. Therefore, in theory, any spiritual transformation (as explained by the hellfire theory) may act as a turning point in an offender's life, leading to desistance from crime.

According to a 2003 Corrections Compendium report, faith based worship services and programs were being offered by all of U.S. prisons. A significant percentage (93%) offered prayer groups (American Correctional Association, 2003). Personal development and parenting classes sponsored by faith based programming were being offered in more than 70% of prison systems reporting to the Compendium (Petersilia, 2004a). The literature on religious programming produced few studies that review its effectiveness in reducing offender recidivism. The few empirical evaluations that do exist provide mixed support for the role that religion plays on prison inmates. A study conducted by Johnson (1984) found that religious prison inmates were no more likely to receive disciplinary confinement than non-religious inmates. In contrast, another credible study found that an inmate's religious participation had a significant and positive impact with respect to prison adjustment (Sumter, 2006).

Empirical research within the prison system suggest that faith based programs can have an effect on prison adjustment. A study by Clear and Sumter (2002) indicate that a significant relationship exists between inmate religiousness and multiple measures of inmate adjustment to the prison environment. Camp et al. (2006) reported that inmates who volunteer to participate in a Life Connections Program established by the Federal Bureau of Prisons were found to be more motivated to make changes in their lives. However a Johnson et al. meta-analysis of 766 studies (2002:11) suggested that "while some support can be found for faith-based interventions of an organic nature (i.e. hypertension, mortality, depression, suicide, promiscuity, substance abuse, and delinquency), research regarding religious programming and well being, self-esteem, and educational attainment is lacking."

There is a consistent and strong relationship between religion and substance abuse. A meta-analysis completed by Johnson, Corbett, and Harris (2001) suggests that over 90% of approximately 100 alcohol and drug studies examined concluded that participation in religious activities was clearly associated with a reduction in alcohol and drug use. This same meta-analysis suggests that people who are frequently involved in religious activities have been diagnosed with reduced risk for depression, and stresses of life (which can also prevent AODA). However, few faith based programs provide long term or sustained services. According to Chaves (1999), the majority of faith based interventions focused on short term and immediate needs. As a result, very little attention was placed on behavioral or other patterns that lead to criminal involvement, which Chaves argues prohibit program evaluation. In addition, faith based organizations frequently collaborate with other organizations (Chaves 2001), making it difficult to determine what was faith based programming or if it even existed within the collaboration. Similarly, it was not always apparent which organizations were actually engaging in religious work or programming that has a religious or spiritual message (Vidal, 2001).

There is mixed empirical research whether religion may be associated with desistence from crime. Burnside *et al.* (2005) suggest that offender programs that have been evaluated to date do not significantly reduce recidivism. Aos et al. (2006) completed a comprehensive review of 291 rigorous evaluations conducted throughout the United States (and other English-speaking countries) and report that some religious programs were found effective in reducing crime, the results were inconclusive regarding faith based programs. Other meta-analyses suggest some relationship or association may exist but more research is needed (Johnson, 2001). Baier and Wright (2001) contend that religious beliefs and behaviors exert a moderate deterrent effect on an individual's criminal behavior. These mixed results might suggest that program implementation and process may have a significant effect on determining outcome measures on reducing criminal activity.

As Petersilia explains, there is no consensus answer to which offender reentry programs work. Petersilia concludes that we know what works in reentry in theory, but that research and practice "are moving on independent tracks and the gulfs between them is still wide" (2004a:8). Petersilia suggests that with more quality evaluations, the more practitioners are able to focus on quality correctional rehabilitative programming. This study hopes to explore or report on faith based treatment in more depth. This being said, religion and religious programming may be one factor that can have an effect on offender reintegration. However, other factors such as the formal and informal social support network an offender has can result in the desistence of AODA and/or criminal behavior.

Case Management and Support Systems

A significant component of the reintegration and/or the aftercare of an offender can be based almost solely on the assisting and monitoring of each offender's successes and failures. Case management and additional monitoring (in addition to having a probation/parole agent) is critical to ensure that the offender is receiving the needed services, is making progress in treatment. This supervision can further reinforce an offender's involvement in the treatment process. Under a brokerage concept, the role of the criminal justice system was limited to referring the offender to the treatment system and subsequently, the treatment system would then independently assess and place the offender in treatment. Therefore, treatment providers and facilitators would be independent and simply provide feedback and progress reports to a probation/parole agent.

Using a more integrated system approach ensures that each offender's treatment is monitored by treatment clinicians, case managers, and criminal justice practitioners. This type of case management integrates substance abuse treatment and intensive probation/parole supervision (Arfken *et al.,* 2003). As Austin and McLelland (1994) explain, a more intensive case management model allows for lower ratios of clients per case manager. This allows for more frequent client contact with the offender while closely monitoring an offender's successes and/or failures.

Case management is almost always utilized in coordination with substance abuse treatment (Sorensen *et al.,* 2003). Case management has been particularly effective with female drug offenders (Siefert and Pimlott, 2001). In their analysis of the Bay Area Services Network (BASN), a parolee services systems model, more contact with case managers significantly predicted fewer days of drug use and fewer property related crimes. Future studies found that there were positive correlations between case management and time in treatment (Longshore *et al.,* 2005).

Case management of drug offenders has been cited as a strategy for service coordination during the transfer of offenders from correctional institutions to communities while also addressing the mental and physical health needs of offenders returning to their communities (Vigilante *et al.,* 1999). Continued community linkages between criminal justice systems and health and human services providers have been found to be very effective (Singer *et al.,* 1995).

Research confirms the importance of regular drug testing of the substance abusing offender as part of an overall strategy to monitor compliance with criminal justice and treatment conditions (Austin and McLelland, 1994). Drug testing should be frequently used with a result quickly available (which is considered a swift compliance gaining strategy). Additionally, the treatment and criminal justice system should share drug testing results to ensure that both are using the compliance gaining strategy. Like other areas previously discussed, resources for drug testing tend to be limited. A team or systems approach is often needed to ensure that offenders are drug tested throughout their treatment programming.

Empirical research indicates that there is a need to involve the community with criminal justice processes, such as correctional reentry. Studies have consistently shown that informal social controls (such as churches, friends and family) can be more powerful than formal agents of control (the police, courts, and corrections) in achieving and maintaining behavior change (Gottfredson and Hirshi, 1990). These informal supports, such as family members were potentially the most powerful community representatives who could be engaged in the reentry process. Very few sources of formal support would likely address the basic survival needs presented to a newly released offender (such as housing, food and clothing, and emotional assistance). Nelson *et al.* (1999:24) suggested that the family plays a significant role in reducing an offender's recidivism rates in their first six months after release from prison.

One of the undeniable aspects of imprisonment is that relationships with family can be strained. Not surprisingly, the increase in incarceration will have consequences for family and children. Almost one half of men and two thirds of women are parents. More than half of U.S. prisoners (55% of state male inmates and 65% of state female inmates) were parents of minor children (Harrison and Beck, 2004:9). By the end of 2002, nearly 2% of all children in America, and 7% of black children had a parent in prison (Harrison and Beck, 2004:6). Including parents who are in jail, on probation and on parole, this number increases to 10% of all children (Mumola, 2002:2). When a parent was sent to prison, the family structure, financial responsibilities, emotional support systems, and living arrangements are all potentially affected. Incarceration, as a result, can drastically disrupt spousal relationships and family networks. Therefore, restoring these relationships and reunifying with the family pose a unique set of challenges.

The burden on both the informal and formal processes has led to the lack of support for the successful reintegration of prisoners. These barriers to reintegration are usually a result of a lack of political, economic or social will. This process of reintegration is perhaps the most widely misunderstood aspect of offenders leaving prison and transitioning back into his/her community. As explained below, many of these programs which have been found to be effective are without funding or underfunded. These support services are integral to assist the millions of offenders in their recovery and re-integrating into their community. Sometimes simple access is difficult to various support networks of government and non-government services in the community.

Housing and Shelter

Safe and securing housing is perhaps the most immediate challenge facing prisoners upon their release. While many returning prisoners have plans to stay with family, those who do not confront limited housing options. The process of obtaining housing is often complicated by a host of factors: the scarcity of affordable and available housing, legal barriers and regulations, prejudices that restrict tenancy for this population, and strict eligibility requirements for federally subsidized housing. Research has found that released prisoners who do not have stable housing arrangements were more likely to return to prison (Métraux and Culhane, 2004). This suggests that there are significant obstacles to secure either temporary or permanent housing.

Housing officials at the city, state, and federal level committed to reversing the rising tide of homelessness have begun to identify prisoner reentry as an issue that requires their attention. In a U.S. Conference of Mayor's Survey on hunger and homelessness, prison release was identified by six cities (Cleveland, Denver, New Orleans, Phoenix, Seattle, and Washington, D.C.) as a major contributor to homelessness (2002). Approximately 13% of those released from prison in 1998 used a homeless shelter within one year of their release (Metraux and Culhane, 2004:12). Another study done of New York State probation/parolee releases found that over half of those who entered a shelter in the first two years after their release from prison did so in the first month (Metraux and Culhane, 2004).

The Travis *et al.* Returning Home study examined the housing arrangements of recently released offenders, as well as the relationship between these arrangements and the successes and challenges of the reentry process. The study found that the majority of returning offenders lived with family members or friends upon release. Three months after release, 88% and 60% of offenders in Illinois and Maryland respectively were living with a family member and/or intimate partner (Travis *et al.*, 2003:18). Many offenders acknowledge that returning home as a living arrangement was only temporary. About 20% of all offenders reported living at more than one address after being in the community for one to three months (Roman and Travis, 2004). Housing options for returning prisoners who do not stay with family members or friends were extremely limited. Potential housing options for former prisoners include community based correctional housing facilities; transitional housing; federally subsidized and administered housing;

homeless assistance supportive housing and special needs housing supported through government services or the private business. The study also found that state department of corrections' personnel felt that there were few evidence based reentry housing programs that targeted returning prisoners with mental illness. Therefore, thousands of persons with mental illness were returning to the community without adequate housing (Roman and Travis, 2004; Travis *et al.,* 2003:13).

According to a number of different studies that examine the demographics of prisoners, the population coming in and out of prison had high rates of homelessness. A Bureau of Justice Statistics study of state prisoners (Mumola, 2000) found that among those state prisoners expected to be released to the community in yearend 1999, 12% reported being homeless at the time of their arrest. The same report validated that 9% of state prison inmates reported living on the street or in a shelter in the 12 months prior to arrest. Looking only at inmates who were mentally ill, the level of homelessness was even higher, nearly 20%.

Studies have also found that offenders reentering into the community are utilizing over-capacity homeless shelter systems. However, the prevalence of homeless shelters was inadequately measured due to poor information gathering. In Roman and Travis' study on homelessness, Riley (2003:2) found that about 800 parolees were in the New York City shelter system on any given day. This represents roughly 3% of the New York City parole caseload. Metraux and Culhane (2004) found that offenders that were homeless at some time in their life were more likely to be homeless after being incarcerated and released. Metraux and Culhane also found that reentry offenders with a history of shelter use were almost five times as likely to have another shelter stay. The same study also found that of New York State prison releases entering homeless shelters sometime after release, 54% did so within the first thirty days (Metraux and Culhane, 2004).

Studies of homeless individuals and families also suggest a relationship between homelessness and time spent in prison or jail. A synthesis of 60 research studies on homelessness conducted in the 1980s found that on average 18% of the population of homeless persons had served time in prison after being convicted of a felony, and about one-third of the population of homeless persons had been jailed for misdemeanor charges (Aos *et al.*, 2006). According to a 1996 National Survey of Homeless Assistance Providers and Offenders, almost half of all homeless adults studied reportedly spent five or more days in a city or county jail, 4% had spent time in a military lock-up, and 18% had been incarcerated in a state or federal prison (Burt *et al.,* 1999:32).

The process of securing housing may be further complicated by the returning prisoner's ineligibility for food stamps, veteran's benefits, and benefits through the Temporary Assistance for Needy Families (TANF) program. Anyone with a drug conviction was barred for life from obtaining food stamps and TANF benefits, unless a state modifies or eliminates this prohibition (Koyanagi, 2002). Other guidelines restrict the use of TANF funds for housing services. The U.S. Department of Health and Human Services (DHHS) considers any TANF funded housing subsidy that was not short term as assistance, even if families were working and not receiving TANF cash benefits. Therefore, a TANF funded housing subsidy provided for more than four months counts against the family's federal lifetime benefit limit (Sard and Waller, 2002:16). Returning prisoners not able to access TANF may be able to obtain other benefits such as Supplemental Security Income (SSI) and Social Security Disability Insurance (SSDI). However, when an individual was incarcerated for more than a month, these benefits were suspended. Upon release from prison, it may take weeks to reinstate these benefits (Koyanagi, 2002).

For a majority of returning prisoners, their first home post release may be with a family member, a close friend, or a significant other. The Vera Institute of Justice study found that of the 49 offenders followed after their release from prison, over 40 were living with a relative, or with their spouse or partner, in the month right after they were released (Nelson *et al.,* 1999:54).

In an Urban Institute's Returning Home study in Maryland, 153 respondents were interviewed about two months after their release. When asked where they went after getting out, nearly half (49%) said they slept at a family member's home their first night. Another 10% slept at a friend's house the first night out of prison. After two months within the community, 80% of offenders reported living with a family member (Roman and Travis, 2004). For some returning prisoners, residing in the home of a family member, friend, or significant other may not be an option. This may have been the result of family conflict, the reluctance of family members to welcome a violent individual back into their lives, or the lack of an immediate family. In other cases there were additional legal restrictions involved. Conditions of parole may have prohibited returning prisoners from residing with a family member or close friend if that individual had a criminal history. According to a 1988 survey of conditions placed on former prisoners under parole supervision, 31 of the 51 responding parole agencies reported that they prohibited parolees from associating with anyone who had a criminal record (Rhine *et al.,* 1991:62).

For those returning prisoners who did not live with loved ones or friends upon release, the housing options could include community based correctional housing (Roman and Travis, 2004). These facilities may include: half-way or three-quarter housing, transitional housing, federally subsidized (voucher) and administered housing, homeless assistance supportive housing and special needs housing. These can also be supported through the U.S. Department of Housing and Urban Development (HUD) and private or non-profit businesses. However, with additional financial and budgetary strain of correctional agencies, these facilities are often full and/or overcrowded.

Many state departments of corrections employ halfway houses to assist offenders reentering into the community from prison. An evaluation by Seiter (1975) in Ohio compared 236 halfway house offenders to a 404 offender parolees. Seiter's study compared recidivism rates based on the severity and frequency of criminal offenses in addition to also using a score of "relative adjustment"; which was a measure of positive activities, such as finding and holding a job, being self supporting, and participating in self improvement programs (1975:249). The group living in a halfway house performed better on positive activities, but not at a statistically significant level. However, those offenders living in a halfway house group were found to have committed less severe and fewer criminal offenses over a period of one year. A Dowell *et al.* study examined a women's halfway house in California. Using a comparison group of parolees, the study indicated that those female offenders who did not live in a halfway house were twice as likely to commit a crime. In addition, offenders who were not living in a halfway house were also more likely to commit more severe crimes (Dowell, 1985:21).

Health Care

The population moving through correctional facilities in the United States presents serious health problems. Interestingly, a period of incarceration often has positive consequences for the health status of an offender because adequate health care is constitutionally required, but also because the food and living environment are more conducive to better health outcomes than many situations in the community.

The overlap between the public health population and the criminal justice population is striking. For example, as Hammett (2001:1) suggests, nearly one-quarter of all people living with HIV or AIDS, one-third living with Hepatitis C, and one-third with tuberculosis in the United States were released from jail or prison in 1997. This data suggests that correctional facilities have the ability to provide access to large numbers of people posing serious public health risks.

The vast majority of offenders released from prison do not have any form of medical insurance. Securing health care has been a major concern for many released offenders. Over three-quarters of offenders in a Returning Home study acknowledged they would need assistance in getting health care (Travis *et al.*, 2003). The study found that between 30% and 40% of offenders reported having a chronic physical or mental health condition, with the most commonly reported conditions including depression, asthma, and high blood pressure (Travis *et al.*, 2003). However, many corrections agencies lack any discharge planning and preparation to addressing the health care needs of offenders upon release. This makes continuity of care extremely difficult. Less than 10% of Illinois offenders reported receiving referrals to health care or mental health care services in the community. It was found that Illinois offenders who reported having between fair and good health were no more or less likely to receive a referral to a community based health care facility than offenders reporting to be in good general health (Travis *et al* , 2003).

Mental Health

Inmates with mental illness are also increasingly being imprisoned and ultimately being released. In 1998, a Bureau of Justice Statistics report estimated that 16% of those incarcerated reported either a mental condition during an overnight stay in a mental hospital (Ditton, 1999). There are relatively few public mental health services available, and studies indicate that even when they are available, mentally ill individuals fail to access available treatment because they fear institutionalization, a denial that they are mentally ill or basic distrust of the mental health system (Lurigio, 1996). Untreated mentally ill people may have a higher tendency to engage in self medication and/or criminal behaviors that eventually lead to arrest and conviction.

A significant percentage of offenders have co-occurring rates of mental health conditions, physical illness and co-morbidity substance abuse (Ditton, 1999). A study by Belenko (2003) found that 32% of inmates with a history of regular drug use and 28% of alcohol involved inmates had indications of a mental health problem. Offender treatment retention studies had found that mental health disorders are predictive of early termination. This would suggest that offenders who need treatment the most do not enter into treatment, nor do they continue their progress to potential recovery.

Although prevalence of mental illness is very difficult to estimate, it appears that schizophrenia, psychosis, major depression, bipolar disorder, and posttraumatic stress disorder were more common among inmates than in the overall U.S. population (NCCHC, 2002). According to a survey conducted by the Bureau of Justice Statistics, almost a third (31%) of state inmates and almost a quarter (23%) of federal inmates reported having a physical or mental health problem (Maruschak and Beck, 2001:5).

Employment and Vocational Training

Research suggests that when people who are released from prison or jail return to the community have poor job prospects and even poorer chances of finding their own place to live. Steurer *et al.* (1999) conducted a three state study on recidivism and found that fewer than half of all released offenders had a job lined up upon their return to the community. This places a larger burden on workforce investment boards, one stop centers, and other publicly financed employment and job training services whose purpose was charged with lowering unemployment. Some of these organizations may be beginning to appreciate the captive audience that this population provides for education and job training. Just one-third (35%) of those released from prison participated in educational programs while incarcerated; even fewer (27%) took part in vocational training (Steurer *et al.*, 2001:52). These low figures are especially troubling when considering that a much greater percentage of the prison population used to receive programming.

Finding and maintaining a job is a critical dimension of successful prisoner reentry. Substantial research indicates that employment was associated with lower rates of recidivism (Bloom *et al.*, 1990). Offenders being released from prison face tremendous challenges in finding and maintaining legitimate job opportunities which can include illiteracy, low levels of education, limited work experience, and limited vocational skills. Also to be taken into account was the general reluctance of employers to hire offenders due to stigmatization and unfair labeling.

Travis *et al.* (2003) identify several issues and barriers related to offender release from prison. The Urban Institute study found significant barriers to offenders being released. While offenders acknowledged that having a part time or full time job was an important factor in staying out of prison, very few offenders (less than 20%) reported having been prepared to look for employment. The study also found that case management could further increase the likelihood of finding and maintaining employment after release from prison. This Opportunity to Succeed (OPTS) evaluation found that participants who interacted with their case manager were more likely to report full-time employment and maintain employment for a longer time than those receiving no case management. Offenders who did manage to find work after release (less than 20%) had significant difficulties in maintaining a consistent employment pattern.

Employment problems can also affect long term recovery and complicate community transition (Belenko and Peugh, 2005). Released offenders with few marketable skills and limited job opportunities were more susceptible to relapse and resumption of illegal activity (Travis *et al.,* 2001). Furthermore, for many inmates, their physical or mental health problems make it difficult for them to sustain employment or successfully complete educational programs (Belenko, 2002). Therefore, in many systems approaches, an effective reentry strategy was to identify an offender's employment and training needs to enable the offender to be reintegrated into the legitimate labor market (Martin and Inciardi, 1993).

Researchers also need to consider that transportation (by car, bus, train) is in itself a potential barrier to employment. In the Opportunity to Succeed (OPTS) evaluation, more than one-third of the offenders reported having difficulty obtaining a car for work or emergencies and nearly a quarter reported various difficulties accessing public transportation. Despite these concerning statistics, the larger Returning Home study found that maintaining employment could reduce recidivism. As levels of employment increased, there were reductions in property, drug and violent crimes (Travis *et al.*, 2003:41).

Correctional agencies across the country envision assisting offenders find employment using vocational training. A review of the literature finds that vocational education programs are effective in reducing offender recidivism. Based on the Sherman *et al.* review (1997), several rigorous studies found that vocational education programs provided in prison or residential settings have reduced the recidivism of its participants. Less rigorous studies have found more general and mixed results. A Saylor and Gaes (1997) study found that significant training could affect both in-prison (misconduct reports) and post prison (employment and arrest rates) outcome measurements. A 1994 Bloom *et al.* evaluation of the Job Training Partnership Act (JTPA) was one of the most rigorous evaluations done on vocational training. Bloom *et al.* (1994) found that offenders who participated in training had higher recidivism rates than those offenders in comparison groups. This particular study highlights the inability to determine why a program was successful with some offenders and not with others. A program was generally determined to be a success was based on whether the majority of offenders were assisted and whether the program reduced their recidivism. If the majority of offenders were not found to reduce recidivism, it was easier for researchers to simply say the program was ineffective.

While the future may seem bleak, employers seeking to retain employees have found that offenders are more than capable and accountable for tardiness, absence, illicit drug use, or irresponsible behavior, which is likely due to the monitoring and surveillance of their probation and parole officers and the conditions of release they enforce. A review of the literature often does not account for why these employment and vocational programs are found to be ineffective. Perhaps it is because we have difficulty rationalizing some of the issues that offenders may face when simply applying for a job. How many offenders have a social security card? Offenders may have memorized their ten digit number, but how difficult is it to replace a social security card if it has been lost? How difficult is it to obtain a drivers license or photo identification? How difficult is it to obtain a copy of a birth certificate? What are the indirect costs of attaining these forms and documents to simply prove your own identity or be eligible for food stamps or a food bank? How about clothing? How many offenders have never owned new clothing? How often do they go to shelters and are told they have to wear something smaller or bigger? How many offenders can afford hygiene products? When was the last time this person had a healthy meal not from a soup kitchen? How about a contact number you can be reached at? This would imply you have the money to afford a phone line or cellular phone. Sometimes we take these for granted because we have access or monetary means to get something done.

Education

There are mixed results in the programming of educational attainment. Vito and Tewksbury (1999) evaluated the Learning, Instruction, and Training Employment (LITE) program in Kentucky, whose purpose was to increase literacy levels of state and local inmates, while indirectly trying to reduce re-arrest. The study identified 662 offenders for program entry. Of those offenders, only 105 offenders participated in and/or completed the six week program. Although offenders that graduated from the program had increased their reading and math competencies, the educational component did not seem to have an effect on offender recidivism rates [when compared to non-graduates after fifteen months] (Vito and Tewksbury, 1999). Another study conducted by Adams *et al.* (1994) reviewed the prison behavior and post-release recidivism of more than 14,000 Texas offenders, where only a small percentage participated in prison education programs. Between 1991 and 1992, after 14 to 36 months, those offenders who participated in prison education showed increases in academic achievement, but their recidivism rates were only affected if the offender participated in 200 or more hours of educational programs (Adams *et al.*, 1994).

As explained above, there are significant obstacles that most offenders face when they are released from jail and/or prison. As Joan Petersilia argues, reentry can be related to both the process of offender incarceration and an offender's post prison experience. Petersilia and Travis (2001) propose reentry as a philosophy and a process which would be inevitably difficult to conceptualize and operationalize. Petersilia and Travis (2001) assert that it was already difficult to operationally define and isolate reentry programs distinctly from the entire correctional system. Consequently, it would be even more difficult to evaluate its effectiveness. Seiter and Kadela (2003) faced a similar dilemma in their recent article, "What Works in Prisoner Reentry?" Therefore, there is no one cookie- cutter aggregate approach of an offender's reentry process. Perhaps this is why many research papers focus so heavily on offender recidivism.

RECIDIVISM

There are several measurements employed to measure offender recidivism. Research by prominent scholars have argued that recidivism can be measured using probation and parole violations, absconding from the criminal justice system, re-arrest, re-conviction, and re-incarceration (Clear *et al.*, 2001; Taxman and Cherkos, 1995; Petersilia, 1998). Estimates of recidivism often vary with the length of the follow up period and the different measurements selected. Re-arrest refers to any arrest for a felony or serious misdemeanor. Re-conviction refers to a conviction on at least one charge after the date of release from prison. Re-incarceration refers to either an offender's return to prison or any new admission to a local jail or prison with a sentence for a new offense. Although much has been written on probation recidivism, there has been considerably less written on the specific violations of probationers while under community supervision.

Repeat offenders or churners are those that have a history of criminal behavior, including offenses that affect the quality of life of the communities. Nearly 60% of federal offenders and 83% of the state prisoners have at least one prior criminal conviction (Beck and Harrison, 2001). The classification issues regarding repeat offender's present significant challenges to correctional administrators. A current offense may be misleading because it may not detail the offender's criminal history or their pattern of criminal behavior. For example, more offenders are in prison for public disorder offenses (an increase of 114% in the last ten years) but their incarceration may be more likely due to their criminal history than the nature of the instant offense. Lynch and Sabol (2001) argue that offenders in prison with violent offenses that were unattended were likely to have behaviors that would carry over into the community. Therefore, due to the nature of an offender's criminal history, research suggests that more attention would be needed to identify typologies of offenders.

Probation and Parole Technical Violations

Studies of probation often report the failure rates of probationers, whereas comparatively little is reported about the specific behaviors (or events) that led to probation failure (Petersilia, 1998). Examinations of the time from commitment to probation to any violations, including new crimes that occur while a probationer serves his or her sentence, were equally scarce. The current study bridges some of these gaps in the literature by providing detail as to the prevalence and timing of these probation and/or parole violations.

The nature of probation violations has significantly impacted our understanding of the needs of the probationer and the supervising functions of probation officers. Clear and Latessa (1993) examined violations in the form of minor rules, major rules, minor offenses, major property offenses, major violent offenses, and drugs/weapons offenses during one and two year intervals in six sites across the United States. Clear and Latessa (1993) found that one-quarter of probationers had violations recorded. Major rule violations accounted for more than one-third of all of the noted offenses; whereas, minor offenses accounted for less than one-third, and all other rule infractions or new crimes accounted for the remaining one-third.

Studies have reported that between one-quarter and one-half of all probationers comply with the terms of their probation (Taxman and Cherkos, 1995). Those who committed a new offense while being supervised, or violated their court orders at least once, also compose a significant proportion of the probation population. It has been reported that technical violations constitute the most common type of violation, followed by major and minor violations (Sims and Jones, 1997).

Trends in probation account for more than half of the total growth in the correctional population since 1990. Overall, the correctional population increased by nearly 2.5 million or 57% of which probationers accounted for 53% of the growth (or 1,492,000). Of all probationers, approximately 70% were under some form of correctional supervision in 2005 (Glaze and Bonczar, 2006:3). The percentage of probationers required to report regularly declined steadily, from 79% in 1995 to 70% in 2005. About 1 in 10 persons still on probation had absconded. Almost 60% of the more than 2.2 million adults discharged from probation in 2005 had successfully met the conditions of their supervision.

According to the Bureau of Justice Statistics, the successful completion rate of probation has dropped from 74% in 1986 to 60% in 1990 (Glaze, 2003:2). This drop in the successful completion of probation sentences may be due to more stringent conditions of probation and/or parole orders that increase the chances for violations. Taxman and Cherkos (1995) have argued that the successful completion of probation can occur despite serious, or numerous technical violations which may have been committed.

Consistent with these findings, Cunniff (1991) and the National Association of Criminal Justice Planners (NACJP) found that approximately one-third of probationers who were successfully discharged did not fully satisfy the conditions of their probation. According to Cunniff (1991), more than half of offenders were not in compliance with their court orders while on probation. Both studies (the Bureau of Justice Statistics and the NACJP) present findings that indicate: (i) more than one-third of probationers receiving treatment made no progress or failed to satisfy their court orders, (ii) one-third of probationers required to submit to drug testing made no progress or failed to satisfy their court orders, (iii) more than one-third of probationers required to perform community service made no progress or failed to satisfy their court orders, and (iv) one-quarter of probationers ordered to pay fines paid nothing or only slightly more than one-third of the total assessed fees (which can include restitution, court costs, or probation/parole costs).

Regarding probation violations, Landis *et al.* (1969) discovered that 80% of probation failures in California were for violations of probation orders, whereas one-fifth were for convictions for new offenses. Langan and Cunniff (1992) found that 62% of probationers in their study had disciplinary hearings for probation violations or were re-arrested. These findings point to the prevalence of violations by probationers. Violators of probation and parole represent the fastest growing category of admissions to corrections facilities, and state leaders agree that this course must be reversed (Blumstein and Beck, 1999). Within three years of being released, over half (52%) are expected to return to prison for either a new crime or parole violation (Langan and Levin, 2002:2). By some measures, the process of prisoner reentry has become much worse than it once was. In 1984, 70% of parolees successfully completed their parole term. By 2002, that number had dropped to 45% (Langan and Levin, 2002:2).

From 1990 to 2002, the state parole population had grown at a slower rate than state prison populations. A large contributor to this can perhaps be the technical violations of parolees. Since 1990, the state prison population nearly doubled, increasing from 708,393 in 1990 to 1,277,127 at year end 2002 (Glaze and Palla, 2004:3). The rate of growth in the prison population slowed between 1999 and 2001, due in part to a rise in the number of releases from prison (592,000 in 2001). Relative to the prison population, the growth in the state parole population was much more modest, increasing from 502,134 in 1990 to 670,169 by 2002 (Glaze and Palla, 2004:3).

Of all 784,408 adult men and women were on parole in 2005, approximately 1 in every 286 adults in the United States were under supervision (Glaze and Bonczar, 2006:2). Almost 37% of all parolees were convicted of a drug offense. Approximately 45% of all parolees successfully met the conditions of their supervision. Since 1995 the total estimated number of parolees discharged from supervision increased to 503,800 in 2005. Between 1995 and 2005, the number of offenders who successfully completed their parole decreased to 227,600 (Glaze and Bonczar, 2006:4).

The rate of parole violations have increased significantly over recent years. In 1985, nearly 70% of parolees successfully completed their parole term and by 1997, that number had dropped to 44% (Glaze, 2003:7). Conversely, the percentage of those who fail on parole has increased from less than a third of all parolees in 1985 to 54% in 1997 (Petersilia, 1999:212). Almost 9% of all parolees nationally were designated as absconding; meaning their whereabouts were unknown to parole agents (Bonczar and Glaze, 1999:5).

The rise in rates of parole failures in conjunction with an increasing base of probation and parole populations had a significant impact on the nation's prison population. In 1980, parole violators constituted 18% of prison admissions; whereas today, they constitute over 37% of prisoners. In 1998, this meant that 207,000 of the 565,000 people admitted to prison were parole violators; individuals who had either been returned to prison on a technical violation or for committing a new offense (Beck, 2000:4). The combination of this increase with the leveling off of new prison commitments from new convictions means that parole revocations are now a significant factor in the rising prison populations.

The collapse of a systematic sentencing philosophy has resulted in enormous state variation in correctional systems resulting in differences in probation and parole practices. For example, in California, 65% of the individuals admitted to prisons in 1997 were parole violators, while in Florida, parole violators accounted for 12% of new admissions (Petersilia,

1999:82). Nationally, parole violators serve on average another five months in prison (Austin, 2001). This is leading to a churning philosophy of probation and parole. Prisons are becoming a revolving door. More people are going to prison under differing sentencing philosophies and returning to their communities which do not have effective systems of reintegration that return these same offenders back to prison.

Arrest, Conviction and Incarceration

Studies of recidivism have concluded that aggregate re-arrest was the most reliable measurement of recidivism, because it is the most likely to be reported (Maltz, 1984). Although some re-arrested individuals may be innocent of the crime charged, using only reported convictions would subsequently understate recidivism rates because not all offenders are prosecuted and/or go to trial. For example, parolees often do not face prosecution for a new offense, but rather their parole may be revoked and the offender may return to prison to serve the balance of their sentence. Therefore, even new convictions may not be an accurate measurement of recidivism. Maltz (1984) and other prominent scholars (Petersilia, 2004b; Sherman *et al.,* 1997) have argued that it would be necessary to use the triangulation of sources and indices to understand the complexity of recidivism (from re-arrest to re-incarceration).

In 1983, the first of two national studies on recidivism were completed by the Bureau of Justice Statistics (BJS). The study examined approximately 16,000 of the nearly 108,580 offenders released from prisons in eleven states in 1983. These offenders represented more than half of all released state prisoners that year. An estimated 62.5% were re-arrested for a felony or serious misdemeanor within 3 years, 46.8% were re-convicted, and 41.4% returned to jail or prison (Beck and Shipley, 1989:2). However, before their release from prison, the offenders had been arrested and charged with an average of more than twelve offenses each, which suggests that many of these offenders were churners throughout the criminal justice system. Nearly two-thirds of offenders had been arrested at least once in the past for a violent offense and two-thirds of offenders had previously been in jail or prison before their most recent release (Beck and Shipley, 1989).

The second national recidivism study in 1994 was a follow up of the 1983 Bureau of Justice Statistics study, which found similar results in offender recidivism. The BJS study utilized four measures of recidivism: re-arrest, re-conviction, re-incarceration of an offender to prison, and the return of an offender to prison with or without a new sentence. The 1994 follow up recidivism study tracked 272,111 offenders for a period of three years after their release. These 272,111 represented approximately two-thirds of all offenders that were released in the United States in 1994. Langan and Levin report that within the first six months of an offender's release, approximately 30% of the 272,111 offenders were re-arrested for a felony or a serious misdemeanor (2002:1). When examining re-arrest over a three year period, the study found that within the first year the cumulative total grew to 44% and within the first two years almost 60%. By the third year of tracking offenders, an estimated 67.5% of the 272,111 released prisoners were re-arrested (at least once). Within the first 3 years of the release of the 272,111 offenders, approximately 22% were re-arrested for a violent offense, 32% for a property offense, 30%, for a drug offense and 28% for a public order offense (Langan and Levin, 2002:4).

Offender re-conviction rates followed a similar trend to re-arrest. Within the first year of an offender's release, approximately 22% of the 272,111 released offenders were re-convicted for a new misdemeanor or felony. After two years, a combined total of 36.4% of offenders were re-convicted. After three years, approximately 47% of offenders released were re-convicted of a misdemeanor or felony (Langan and Levin, 2002:5).

The 1994 national study also examined offender re-incarceration in more depth. Over one-quarter of offenders released in 1994 had returned to either a state or federal prison as a result of another prison sentence (due to violating their probation/ parole or a new criminal activity). This does not include offenders that were sentenced to jail time. Of the quarter of offenders re-incarcerated, over half (52%) of offenders were re-incarcerated because they had violated a technical condition of their release, such as failing a drug test, missing an appointment with their parole officer. Approximately 48% of offenders were re-incarcerated because they had committed a new misdemeanor or felony crime (Langan and Levin, 2002:4-6).

Langan and Levin (2002) also reported that different categories of offenders (particularly property offenders) had different rates of recidivism. Despite only one-third of all released offenders incarcerated were perpetrators of a property offense, statistics indicated that released property offenders had higher recidivism rates than those released for violent, drug, or public order offenses. An estimated 74% of the property offenders released in 1994 were re-arrested within three years, compared to 62% of the violent offenders, 67% of the drug offenders, and 62% of the public order offenders (Langan and Levin, 2002:14). Research indicated that property offenders also had higher rates of re-conviction and re-incarceration than other types of offenders.

Comparing the 1983 and 1994 national studies on recidivism, Langan and Levin (2002:8) note that only offender re-arrest rates had risen. The overall re-arrest rate rose sharply between 1983 and 1994. In 1983, 62.5% were re-arrested within 3 years and of the 272,111 released in 1994, re-arrest increased to 67.5%. This re-arrest statistic held definitively for all released offenders. Property offenders arrest rates increased from 68% to 74% respectively (Langan and Levin, 2002:6). Released violent offenders recidivism rates had a relatively small increase of 60% to 62% between 1983 and 1994 (Langan and Levin, 2002:8). Released drug offenders increased from 50% to 67% respectively. Released public order offender recidivism rates for arrest also increased from 55% to 62%. Between 1983 and 1994, the overall offender re-conviction rate did not increase significantly, remaining at approximately 47% (Langan and Levin, 2002:8).

Similarly, there were no significant changes for released property, violent or public order offenders. The only significant change in re-conviction rates between 1983 and 1994 was for drug offenders. Among drug offenders released in 1983, 35% were re-convicted for a new crime (not necessarily another drug offense). Among those released in 1994, the re-conviction percentage was significantly higher at 47% (Langan and Levin, 2002:8).

SYSTEMS BASED APPROACH

Seiter and Kadela (2003:4) defined a good reentry program as either a program based on the transition from prison to community or a program that provides a continuity of treatment from the prison setting and community programming. This process is both situational and individualistic as each person responds to their own environment in a unique way. Therefore, we should also expect that how we study and measure success and failure can be based on each individual researcher's perspective. Below are a variety of perspectives and studies of correctional reentry from Robert Martinson's controversial work to a system based approach that stresses the coordination of government and non-government agencies to assist offenders returning from prison.

Martinson

In 1974, Robert Martinson, an assistant professor at the City College of New York, published an article titled "What Works? Questions and Answers about Prison Reform" (Martinson, 1974). His article summarizes 231 offender rehabilitation programs over a period of thirty years. Based on Martinson's analysis, which he explains as the Effectiveness of Correctional Treatment (ECT), he concludes that "with few and isolated exceptions, the rehabilitative efforts that have been reported so far have had no appreciable effect on recidivism" (1974:25). Martinson's article has been cited as a significant factor in increasing the skepticism of the rehabilitation, treatment, and medical movement of corrections in the 1970s and 1980s. This study inadvertently created a controversy which led to more research on offender recidivism.

Martinson (1974) argued that there was very little evidence of success of rehabilitative programs in his ECT evaluation. These programs included: educational and vocational training, individual counseling, group counseling, and psychotherapy. Martinson determined that this ineffectiveness was due to both the integrity of program implementation and a bias in how these programs were evaluated. Martinson uses the evaluation research to argue that the weakness of program implementation was undermined (Visher *et al.*, 2004). For example, many studies' methodologies focused on experimental designs in which Martinson found that sub-samples of the experimental group (rather than the entire experimental group) saw reductions in recidivism. Martinson argued that "some of the treatment programs are working to some extent, but that the research is so bad that it is incapable of telling" (1974:49). Martinson further argued that there was a relationship between the treatment providers who offer offender services and evaluators who set out to prove the effectiveness of such programming meaning that this relationship could lead to biased results.

In 1979, Martinson followed up his previous ECT meta-analysis by essentially recanting his previous position. Martinson argued that "some treatment programs do have an appreciable effect on recidivism" (1979:244). Martinson further argued that he had not utilized all correctional studies because he felt they did not meet specific methodological standards. This would suggest that Martinson may have lowered his threshold for defining effectiveness rather than alter his views based on more compelling evidence.

Martinson has been highly criticized for his studies on offender rehabilitation (Sherman *et al.,* 1997). However, Martinson does make several valid statements arguing that researchers and evaluators may be guilty of dramatizing the effectiveness of programs for the betterment (sustainability) of a program.

This author finds some fault in Martinson's argument in that most programs are considered deficient or unsuccessful at a particular aggregate percentage, which makes it easy for people to inherently criticize. For instance, if a student receives 10% on an exam, would that be celebrated? What about 40%? Is that a good measurement of the student's skills and performance? Might this be a result of poor teaching and instruction? Or perhaps this was a poorly validated measure for the teacher and/or student. What percentage is good enough? What chi-square value is really exceptional? At what level of confidence? These are all in the eyes of each researcher. Is it process or impact evaluations that are more important? Some studies choose to exemplify what others do not. Some researchers choose qualitative over quantitative research. Today, we consider more cost-benefit analyses. These are all issues that may have opened the hearts and minds of many academics, practitioners and legislators wanting to learn and educate more on this black box of recidivism.

Post-Martinson

Scholars from different disciplines continue to dispute Martinson's 1974 findings and subsequently, have generated data on the effectiveness of offender rehabilitation programs.

Successful challenges to Martinson's research were generated by Gendreau and Ross. Gendreau and Ross (1979) preferred to examine success based on individual offender outcomes rather than aggregating percentages of what definitely worked or did not work. In the view of the psychologists, it was necessary to examine the accomplishments of the principles of the program (process) rather than simply examining outcome measurements.

Using a variety of techniques, including narrative reviews and meta-analyses, Gendreau and Ross developed a list of principles of effective intervention. Gendreau and Ross's findings suggested that recidivism was possible and that the effectiveness of treatment programs could vary substantially on the individual offender (age, prior record, etc.). Their findings confirmed that evidence based principles of risk, need, and response are useful. Gendreau and Ross (1979) identified treatment services that employ both behavioral and cognitive social learning techniques of modeling, role playing, reinforcement, extinction, resource provision, verbal suggestions, and cognitive restructuring. Services should be intensive, lasting between three and twelve months (depending on need) while occupying 40% to 70% of the offender's time during the course of the program (Cullen and Gendreau, 2000:29). This was intended to target high risk offenders' criminogenic needs. Less hardened or lower risk offenders may not require this intense intervention.

An Andrews and Bonta (1998) evaluation of correctional programs found that the most effective and reliable intervention were cognitive behavioral programs. Based on the deficiencies of each offender, these cognitive behavioral programs would define the problems that led offenders into conflict, identify goals, generate alternatives, and implement various solutions (Andrews and Bonta, 1998). This approach was also found to be effective by Gendreau and Ross (1979); whose studies found that control based programming that deter offenders through surveillance and threats of punishment were ineffective.

Between 1978 and 1998, MacKenzie and Hickman (1998) identified 184 correctional evaluations that employed a rigorous methodology, which they termed a level three, meaning that each study employed some form of experimental design or comparison group). MacKenzie and Hickman's analysis found that in-prison therapy followed with community treatment, cognitive behavioral therapy, community based sex offender treatment, vocational education, multi component correctional industry, and community employment programs were the most effective in reducing recidivism. The study also identified studies in which MacKenzie and Hickman felt were promising (defined as one or two evaluations that indicated effectiveness). These promising programs were prison based sex offender treatment, adult education and any transitional programs that assisted high risk offenders in employment preparation. The

MacKenzie and Hickman study also found that increased surveillance and monitoring in the community did not alone reduce recidivism.

Pearson and Lipton reviewed both published and unpublished correctional treatment studies conducted between 1968 and 1996. Pearson and Lipton (1999) examined different domains of treatment such as: therapeutic communities (TC), group counseling, education, vocational training, mentoring and boot camps. A review of treatment and counseling modalities found that most of the programming was found to be ineffective. These programs included life skills education, correctional industry programs, work programs, psychosocial sex offender treatment, domestic violence treatment, boot camps, and intensive scared straight supervision programs. The few programs that were found to be effective were multi-pronged approaches that centered on skill oriented cognitive behavior (Pearson and Lipton, 1999).

Seiter and Kadela's evaluation of both published and unpublished literature between 1975 and 2001 identified that only 28 program evaluations met a reentry definition (as specified previously). Of all programs, only 19 studies utilized a quasi experimental group (meeting a level three criteria). Only two of these evaluations were randomized experiments. Their 2003 study brings to light a significant issue within correctional research throughout a twenty five year period. Hundreds of programs were either poorly evaluated or lacked the design to establish a reliable conclusion. However, based on the meta-analysis, Seiter and Kadela (2003) identified vocational training and work release programs, halfway houses, and intensive drug treatment programs with aftercare as programs that generated reductions in offender recidivism. They also found that education programs increased an offender's education achievement but did not have an effect on recidivism. In addition, Seiter and Kadela also found that pre-release programs were found to be somewhat effective despite the design of the studies.

Many regional organizational studies have argued that a holistic approach to correctional reintegration was necessary for offenders to effectively transition into their communities. Petersilia (1998; 2004a) argues that offender reentry can be simply defined as all activities and programming conducted to prepare ex-convicts to return safely to the community and to live as law abiding citizens. This would include the process of incarceration, how an offender spent their time during confinement, the process by which an offender was released, and how an offender was supervised after release. Based on this philosophy, Petersilia (2004a) argues that successful offender reentry could be accomplished through a relationship between an offender's reentry plan for programming and reintegration, their families, community partnerships, justice professionals, and the victims of the offender's criminal activity (stressing accountability and restorative justice).

What Works, What Doesn't and What's Promising

What has been working? Perhaps the largest and most influential recidivism study of offender reentry was conducted by Lawrence Sherman and other leading researchers in the field. The U.S. Department of Justice funded report in collaboration with the University of Maryland, What Works, What Doesn't, and What's Promising is perhaps the most well known meta-analysis of offender reentry programs. The researchers assessed the quality of the research methods of more than 500 studies of various crime prevention programs. The researchers used a two-step procedure for drawing conclusions about what works in crime prevention. The first step was to assess the quality of the research design and methodology of each study. For the most part, each of the studies reviewed were conducted within the last 10 years.

Sherman *et al.* (1997) examined the scientific rigor of each study from its research design, selection problems, attrition, statistical analysis, statistical controls, and sample size. Rigor scores were given to each study which ranged from one (no rigor) to five (most rigorous). A level five study design would include random assignment, and an analysis of a comparable program and/or comparison groups, which can include controls for attrition. The second step was to examine the significance of each study's results. After a synthesis of reviews, Sherman *et al.* (1997) found that there was a dilemma between design rigor and the number of studies that were utilized. Therefore, researchers identified studies with a scientific rigor score of three or more that could be used to draw conclusions about what works, what does not, what was promising, and what was unknown.

Sherman's evidence based policing (1999) proposed the paradigm that decision making should be based on the strength of the evidence. Associating this paradigm to corrections would argue that evidence based decision making would use research to guide practice and evaluate programs. The goal would be to use scientific evidence to hold officials, practitioners and researchers accountable for their practices. Sherman would argue that academics and practitioners should focus and concentrate their efforts on determining what works and make commitments to increasing program efficacy. Programs that emphasize deterrence, such as shock probation and scared straight programs have been found to be ineffective in reducing AODA offender usage and an offender's criminal behavior (Sherman *et al.*, 1997). Furthermore, any deterrence based programming, which was used as the only instrument to reduce recidivism to emphasize offender discipline has been found to be ineffective. There was no evidence that the correctional boot camps using the old-style military model of discipline, drill, and ceremony were effective methods of reducing recidivism (MacKenzie, 1997).

Many state department of corrections offer programs to offenders that intensify an offender's surveillance in the community. These programs could include: intensive supervised probation or parole, home confinement, community residential programs and urine testing. These tactics, used alone, have been found to be ineffective, if not used in conjunction with other programming. Research identifies that these alternative punishments and sanctions were not effective in reducing recidivism (Petersilia and Turner, 1993). It should be noted, as before, that these programs may become effective if they are combined with AODA treatment or cognitive learning. There was not enough literature to say, with certainty that these programs would be ineffective (Petersilia, 2004a). For example, there were few studies that evaluate the combined effects of both intensive treatment programs and a scared straight program for DUI offenders. Therefore, it would have been difficult to rule out that these programs would be ineffective if combined (Sherman *et al.,* 1997).

It should be accepted, post-Martinson, that many programs are effective in correctional rehabilitation programming. These studies, as do others argue that researchers need to examine program accountability, resource allocation, and various outcome measurements. With more scientifically rigorous methods, recidivism and reentry programs will likely be evaluated with more tenacity, which better determines what was working within the program and what was not. This allows practitioners to change the implementation of the program towards success. One such approach has been the use of an offender's religious background to approach changing one's lifestyle for the betterment of others, rather than simply for selfish and/or personal reasons.

There are a large number of programs utilized that sponsor the collaboration between departments of corrections and other government/ non-government agencies. These initiatives propose building agreements with a variety of government and non-government agencies (i.e. social services) to partner with the Department of Corrections and their facilities in assisting offenders reenter into their communities, while also addressing recidivism.

The Department of Justice funded the Reentry Partnership Initiatives (RPI) in eight sites. Byrne *et al.* (2002), evaluators of RPI, suggest that effective reentry program required a collaborative agency approach between government and the community. The systematic approach to reentry was said to improve public safety, which also required the criminal justice system (police, courts and corrections) to work with the community. Therefore, RPI argues that criminal justice agencies need to redefine their roles and responsibilities. This shifts the focus of these organizations to work collectively and in partnership to improve public safety. RPI programming further involves the shared decision making by police, institutional corrections, community corrections, and public/private service providers.

The National Institute of Corrections' (NIC) Transition from Prison to Community Initiative (TPCI) also identifies the need for the correctional system to create partnerships with the police, court system and communities. Parent (2004) argues that probation and parole agencies must work with social service agencies to form strategic and tactical partnerships to integrate and coordinate basic reentry policies.

The Serious and Violent Offender Reentry Initiative (SVORI) which began in 2002, was designed to develop inmate reentry processes that were focused on public safety. The goals of the SVORI were to increase public safety by reducing recidivism and noncompliance; to improve health by addressing substance abuse and physical and mental health; to improve self-sufficiency through employment, housing, family, and community involvement; and to achieve systems change through multi-agency collaboration and case management (Lattimore *et al.,* 2004).

A study by the Vera Institute of Justice in New York City identified many current issues that confront inmates released from prison (Nelson *et al.,* 1999). The Nelson *et al.* study examined 88 randomly selected inmates released from state prisons. Of those selected, 49 (or 56%) completed the study by allowing interviews to determine their progress and successful transition from prison to the community (Nelson *et al.*, 1999:19). Several issues were identified, including finding housing, creating ties with family and friends, finding a job, alcohol and drug abuse, continued involvement in crime, and the effect of parole supervision (Nelson *et al.,* 1999). Even at the point of release, few offenders within the study were assisted in their initial reentry plans (such as initially being released from prison).

Therefore, many states have developed institutional and/or community based programs have been developed to assist offenders in their reentry into the community.

Administrators of social service systems are beginning to recognize that the demand for treatment and other supports in prison and jail presents opportunities to expand the capacity of their community-based providers. These pressures have pushed corrections administrators, other criminal justice officials, and community-based service providers closer together. A focus on reentry highlights the connections between criminal justice policy and other social policy domains. This was particularly evident for alcohol and other drug abuse (AODA) treatment modalities that are necessary to curb the churning effect that offenders have when cycling in and out of the criminal justice system.

Based on research findings from over 35 years of studies on treatment and the criminal justice system, the systems approach allows for a flexible and integrated service delivery model whereby the criminal justice and treatment systems jointly make decisions on assessment, placement, treatment progress, transition, and support services for offenders. The systems approach continues to evolve from prior collaboration and coordination while building relationships among various agencies to provide needed services (Austin and McLelland, 1994). Researchers and practitioners note that these efforts can fall short to provide sufficient and appropriate substance abuse treatment services due to poor inter-organizational change and communication, a lack of infrastructure, resources, competition, or lack of services. These systems approaches are designed to overcome some of these shortcomings to support better quality treatment programs for each criminal justice offender.

CHAPTER 3:

Methodology of the Study

This chapter examines the current study from research design to the research questions and hypotheses that have been generated from the literature review. The first part of the chapter describes Lake City, the site of the current study. Further discussion focuses on the design of the study and issues related to validity and reliability. Concluding, the researcher discusses the conceptualization and operationalization of the two primary research models that served for the basis of this study.

LAKE CITY

Lake City has used imprisonment as the primary solution to fixing the substance use – crime nexus which has placed a huge burden on the taxpayers. In Lake City, people convicted of nonviolent drug offenses account for over 34% of the recent growth of the city's share of the State prison population (State Department of Corrections, 2004). In Lake City, funding for the *Access To Recovery*'s (*ATR*) state substance abuse treatment infrastructure falls short of meeting the needs of offenders being released from jail and/or prison. From both an economic and public safety perspective, there were significant advantages in developing an *ATR* program which was being studied. A 2003 RAND study estimates that treatment of cocaine addicts reduced serious crime fifteen times more effectively than imprisonment. A 2004 U.S. Department of Health and Human Services (DHHS) study found that decreases in drug use, drug sales and arrests for other crimes were attributable to AODA treatment completion (Barry, 1999). Therefore, any expansion of funding for effective substance abuse treatment, such as the *ATR* program was welcomed.

In fiscal year 2004-2005, the State's Department of Corrections Division of Community Corrections had an annual budget of just $19 million to pay for services needed by probationers and parolees which included housing, day reporting, transportation, drug testing, substance abuse, educational programs and other programming. Halfway houses and transitional living spending was approximately 70% of the 2004-2005 budgets, leaving the State's Department of Corrections (DOC) with roughly $5.5 million, or $82 per offender under supervision, to fund all other services. The total budget for substance abuse treatment in fiscal year 2004–2005 was less than $1.2 million. Over the last half decade, community corrections funding continued to be reduced. In fiscal year 1998-1999, a majority (54%) of DOC expenditures went to adult institutions while 18% was spent on community corrections (State Department of Corrections, 2004). By 2004-2005, funding for adult institutions accounted for 64% of the total budget and community corrections received 14% (Greene and Pranis, 2006: 23).

The growth in the state's prison population has been attributed to the elimination of parole and good time, as well as the dramatic increases in maximum sentences that accompanied truth in sentencing. For example, under the indeterminate system, a person convicted of intent to deliver, selling five grams or less of cocaine faced a prison term of up to 10 years. The offender would be eligible for parole after serving 25% of the prison term (approximately 2.5 years) and reach mandatory release after serving 66% of the prison term (approximately 6.6 years). After Truth in Sentencing (TIS) went into effect, the maximum sentence was raised to 15 years and the maximum term of confinement set at 10 years before being released to a term of extended supervision that might range from a minimum of two and a half years to a maximum of five years.

War on Drugs

The rise in the number incarcerated for nonviolent offenses can be largely attributed to the war on drugs (Greene and Pranis, 2006). Lake City's drug war gained stature in 1990, when the District Attorney's office created a special unit to focus solely on drug prosecutions. Defense attorneys in Lake City have reported that prior to the early 1990s it was common for individuals convicted of small, first time drug sales to be convicted of misdemeanors and placed on probation (Lake City, 2003). When the drug unit was formed, there were around 200 prisoners under DOC supervision who had been sentenced in Lake City Circuit Courts for nonviolent drug offenses. Four years later, however, the number had doubled to nearly 400. By 1998, when Lake City joined the Justice Department's High Intensity Drug Trafficking Area (HIDTA) program, the population had doubled again to more than eight hundred. With increased federal resources, the number of new drug cases and prison admissions continued to increase.

With a rise in both property and violent crime in the last decade, Lake City government officials have continued to pursue drug enforcement strategies, which have directly resulted in the increase of the prison population. A study by local university researchers found that 40% of all Lake City arrestees tested positive for illicit substances, while 34% of arrestees were diagnosed with an alcohol or drug dependency disorder (Lake City, 2003). The study consisted of interviews and voluntary drug tests conducted with arrestees from Lake City and a cross section of counties with medium sized and small cities. The researchers found that alcohol was the most commonly abused substance statewide, but that in Lake City, the majority of arrestees tested positive for one or more controlled substances, most often cocaine (33%) and marijuana (27%).

As drug convictions continue to rise in Lake City, the number of people sentenced to probation fell by 9% between 2000 and 2003 while the number of drug cases sentenced to prison increased substantially by 53% (State Department of Corrections, 2004). The number of nonviolent drug prisoners from Lake City increased by 51% (nearly 700 prisoners) between 1999 and 2004, compared to a 19% increase in the rest of the state. Between 2000 and 2003, the annual number of new drug prisoner admissions from Lake City increased 48%, from 642 to 952. By 2004, Lake City accounted for 58% of the state's drug prisoners (Greene and Pranis, 2006:13).

State Department of Correction data identify that particular crimes have resulted in significant prison growth. The State's Department of Corrections indicate that alcohol and other drug offenses have accounted for a 60% increase of all prison population growth over the last five years (2004:12). Three of the four most frequent offenses that were driving prison admissions were drug crimes according to the State's Sentencing Commission (2002:38). The following were directly connected to substance abuse: (i) possession with intent to deliver (one gram), (ii) possession with intent to deliver (one to five grams), and (iii) operating under the influence.

Racial and Ethnic Disparities

Considered one of the most segregated cities in the United States, Lake City has become a breeding ground of racial and ethnic tension. African Americans and other people of color are incarcerated at higher and more disproportionate rates relative to their share of the *ATR*'s State population (Greene and Pranis, 2006:28). The Sentencing Project (2004) found that this state ranked sixth in a national index of racial disparity in incarceration. The 2004 Report also found that the State had the nation's highest prison and jail incarceration rate for African Americans, almost 4,058 per 100,000 residents. African Americans comprise of 5% of the State's residents while making up almost half (47%) of all of the State's prisoners and nearly two-thirds (64%) of those incarcerated for drug offenses (Greene and Pranis, 2006). Whites make up 89% of the State's residents but less than half of all State prisoners. After more thorough study, African Americans were more likely than whites to be arrested for drug offenses, but the difference was not enough to account for the disparity in incarceration rates.

Arrest data collected by the Office of Justice Assistance's Statistical Analysis Center (SAC) show that African Americans accounted for 27% of all drug arrests in 2003 and 48% of drug sale arrests (Greene and Pranis, 2006:15). When ethnicity was factored in, non-Hispanic whites make up 87% of State residents and comprised of only 43% of prisoners. Latinos accounted for 5% of the State's population comprised of 8% of all sentenced prisoners and 12% of all drug prisoners (Greene and Pranis, 2006:16).

According to the Bureau of Justice Statistics, the State imprisoned nearly 390 people for every 100,000 residents (Sabol *et al.*, 2006:9). However, as stated above, the State's current incarceration prison rates vary widely by race and ethnicity. Non-Hispanic whites were imprisoned at a rate of 196 per 100,000 while Latinos, Native Americans and African Americans were incarcerated at rates of 647 per 100,000, 1,251 per 100,000 and 3,012 per 100,000, respectively (Sabol *et al.*, 2006:10). African Americans in the State were fifteen times more likely to be incarcerated than non-Hispanic whites. The disparity was even greater among those serving time for nonviolent drug offenses. Non-Hispanic whites were incarcerated for nonviolent drug offenses at a rate of just 17 per 100,000. The odds of being incarcerated increased significantly for Native Americans (69 per 100,000); Latinos (157 per 100,000); and African Americans (663 per 100,000). Nearly 1% of the state's African American population was serving time in prison for nonviolent drug offenses (Sabol *et al.*, 2006; Lake City, 2003).

A study by Oliver (2006) argues that there was a significant racial disparity in incarceration in the Lake City jurisdiction. Oliver found that the rate of prison admissions for blacks had increased from 600 per 100,000 residents in the 1990s to over 1,200 per 100,000 in 2005, while the rate of white prison admissions climbed only slightly. Oliver (2006) suggests that the racial disparity in incarceration was not being driven primarily by violent crime but, rather drug crimes.

Over the last 25 years, the State's prison population had grown significantly from less than 4,000 in 1980 to nearly 23,000 today (State Department of Corrections, 2005:4). The State's incarceration rate had increased from 85 prisoners for every 100,000 state residents in 1980 to 390 per 100,000 at the end of 2004. Within the 1990s, the rise in the State's incarceration rate surpassed neighboring states as well as the nation.

Once incarcerated, the State Department of Corrections screening tools had identified almost 83% of inmates who require clinical substance abuse treatment and/or drug education (Lake City, 2003). Nearly 20% of those inmates with substance abuse problems did not receive any AODA services while they were incarcerated because services were unavailable (Lake City, 2003). Based on the Bureau of Justice Statistics Reentry Trends in the United States report, Lake City ranks within the top 25 counties of probation and parole releases (Hughes and Wilson, 2002). Acknowledging that many offenders do not receive treatment due to a lack of participation or services and that the community corrections budget was being reduced annually, *ATR* programming had become a need rather than simply an alternative.

There was no doubt that the capacity of community corrections would be enhanced in Lake City as a result of the *ATR* grant that the State received in March 2004 from SAMHSA. The pilot project was developed in collaboration by the Department of Corrections, State Department of Health and Family Services and the Lake City County Health Division.

RESEARCH DESIGN

The following section explains the design and methodology of the current study. This *ATR* program was evaluated solely on outcome measurements. Therefore, this study focused on the offenders who voluntarily participated in the *ATR* programming in Lake City.

As explained in the literature, there are few studies that have utilized a true experimental design for correctional reentry program evaluation. According to Sherman *et al.* (1997), this should not diminish the results or significance of the study. Based on this perspective, the researcher clearly utilizes a variety of methods to test correctional program effectiveness.

This study utilized a one group one shot treatment design. This experimental design involved the exposure of a group of offenders to a treatment (*ATR* programming), which was further followed by a measurement. This varies from a true experimental design in that there was no control group in which to make comparisons. To complete a more thorough examination of the study, the researcher initially expected to use an experimental design. To do so, it would have been necessary to locate a control group. The researcher completed several applications to the Lake City Department of Corrections and like others, was denied access to offenders released into Lake City who were not participating in the Lake City program. The researcher's expectation was that a large number of offenders would not be eligible for the program or would not want to participate. Fortunately or unfortunately, for the purposes of this study, a large percentage of offenders released chose to take part in the *ATR* program (or continue to remain on a waiting list) which would have resulted in a small pool of eligible control selected offenders. Subsequently, there was no random selection of offenders. In an *ATR* program such as this, it would have been difficult for offenders to not participate in a program that readily assisted them in AODA treatment, housing, clothing, and finding suitable employment (among other extrinsic rewards). The researcher would argue that a significant majority (over 95%) of offenders who were released from the Lake City's Department of Correctional system with a substance abuse issue voluntarily chose the *ATR* programming and were wait-listed.

Internal Review Board (IRB)

For the purposes of this study, it was necessary to get the proposal for the study reviewed by Lake City's Internal Review Board. The proposal met the expectations of the reviewers and the study was approved on May 19, 2006 for a period of one year, as of April 19, 2006. For the purposes of identification, the research study was assigned IRB number 7-2006. It was necessary for the researcher to go through a full board without expedited review because the researcher would be going through case files including aggregate databases developed by agencies implementing the Lake City *ATR* program. Due to the nature of the documentation, it was important for the researcher to specify that all data would be kept confidential and reported only in aggregate.

With any research that utilizing special populations, such as offenders, it was important to sufficiently protect each offender's privacy. Based on the sources of information (explained more thoroughly below), it was necessary to keep each offender's information anonymous and confidential. The researcher made assurances to the Lake City IRB Committee that at no time would the researcher utilize the data in case studies. The information collected would only be used in aggregate, which was sufficient to generate a better understanding of evaluating the *ATR* program while also studying offender recidivism.

Eligibility

Lake City's *ATR* program had several criteria. The offender must have been a resident of Lake City, over eighteen years of age, and met the financial criteria of the State. For an offender to be placed into the program, they must have had self reported and acknowledged an AODA issue. Each offender also had to meet the diagnostic criteria for a substance use disorder. Based on the initial grant proposal, offenders would be eligible for several episodes of *ATR* programming. However, for the purposes of this study, the researcher limited each offender to their first episode of treatment. Specifically, the correctional offenders were re-entering from any prison or prison-bound offenders (of a felony) who had been given this *ATR* program as an alternative to their revocation.

Sample Size

Based on the *ATR*'s Department of Corrections, there were approximately 9,000 offenders that were released from prison in

2005. Of those 9,000 offenders, approximately 30% would reside in the Lake City's jurisdiction. This was estimated based on arrest and conviction rates of offenders during admission to prison facilities. Based on these estimates, approximately 2,700 offenders would be expected to re-enter into Lake City's jurisdiction.

The criteria set forth in the grant application by Lake City, the grant would be expected to service approximately 1,200 people per year in the *ATR* program. Within the SAMHSA grant, 50% of all eligible applicants to the program were to be a part of the criminal justice system. Using these statistics, the general target population for the program would be approximately 600 offenders annually. Between May, 2005 and June, 2006, the researcher accurately determined 434 newly released offenders had received some form of AODA treatment and ancillary services through the *ATR*'s programming. The total number of possible prison released offenders who participated in the Lake City *ATR* program was 456. There were 22 offenders who participated in the program and were not counted. Thirteen offenders had been given a second opportunity at the *ATR* program (and were therefore, disqualified) and nine offender's files were simply inaccurate or invalidated due to a number of factors: unreliable names, a lack of identification, birth date and/or screening documentation.

Sources of Information

The researcher used several sources of information in which to generate a larger database on offenders who participated in the Lake City *ATR* program. For the purposes of the study, it was necessary for offenders to be referred to the program through their probation/ parole agent. Once the referral was completed, the offender was often placed on a wait list to receive a case manager and treatment location of their choosing. Once wait listed, the offender would receive a detailed and in-depth screening which would determine their adequacy of the program. As explained previously, the most basic criteria for access to the program required offenders to self report a problem with alcohol or drug abuse.

Before an offender's initial interview, it was necessary to screen offenders at different stages of the criminal justice system. For that reason, screeners conducted interviews in several locations. Several screeners were dispatched on a daily basis to Lake City jails or State prisons to interview offenders awaiting release. Other screeners would be available to take offender referrals from probation/ parole agents. In addition, there were also experienced screeners accepting applications on a special need, emergency, or expedited basis. Therefore, offenders could be at very different stages of the criminal justice system, and there was no clearly identifiable way for the *ATR* site to determine each type of offender.

During the screening process, each offender would be asked a variety of questions to ensure they would qualify for the alcohol and other drug abuse (AODA) voucher programming. The strength of this particular *ATR* site was that the administration acknowledged that offenders may or may not have received AODA treatment in prison or

within the community. Therefore, there was a possibility that some offenders had already sought treatment before, and others had no understanding of what type of treatment they may receive. Based on the screener's recommendation, each offender would receive some form of AODA treatment: residential (in-patient); intensive outpatient treatment (several times a week); and outpatient (once/ twice a week). These recommendations were made based on two alcohol and drug use assessment tools: the Addiction Severity Index (ASI) and the American Society of Addiction Medicine, second edition, revised Patient Placement Criteria (ASAM PPC-2R). These tools were necessary in examining the nature and scope of the offenders' substance abuse problems, strengths and deficits and domains in an offender's life which could be of issue in recovery and identifying the full range of offender needs for long term sobriety (SAMHSA, 2006).

The Addiction Severity Index (ASI) is the most widely used alcohol and drug assessment tool in the evaluation of substance abuse treatment. The ASI has been established as the standard assessment tool for alcohol and other addictions (Leonard *et al.*, 2000). The ASI was an interview that assesses the history, frequency, and consequences of alcohol and drug use, as well as five additional domains that are commonly associated with drug use: medical, legal, employment, social/family, and psychological functioning. The higher the aggregate score of each component of the ASI, the greater risk an offender faces in each of these areas. Once a screener had determined an offender's ASI score, they were used to profile an offender's problem areas and plan a course of effective, long term treatment (with the assistance of a case manager).

The American Society of Addiction Medicine Second Edition–Revised of Patient Placement Criteria (ASAM PPC-2R), is also a well known assessment tool for placement, continued stay and discharge of offenders with substance abuse. The ASAM was also used because of its strength in determining the scope of co-occurring mental and substance-related disorders (or dual diagnosis). The ASAM outlines five broad levels of care for each type of offender: early intervention, outpatient, intensive outpatient/day treatment, residential, and medical managed intensive inpatient treatment. Within these broad levels of service are criteria based on six dimensions: (i) acute intoxication/withdrawal potential, (ii) biomedical conditions and complications, (iii) emotional, behavioral or cognitive conditions and complications, (iv) readiness to change, (v) relapse, continued use or continued problem potential, and (vi) recovery environment.

In addition to the two screening tools, the interviewer would probe each offender with a variety of questions. First, offenders were expected to identify their real name (aliases), social security number and other demographic information. Once all information was documented, the interviewer would assist the offender in choosing both their treatment options (type of treatment available and various agencies) and the agency in which they will work with for case management. It should be noted that all information presented to the screener could have been falsified due to the self report nature of the subject. Therefore, a review of each offender's case manager's case notes was needed to adequately verify the reliability and validity of the self report information.

Once offenders were screened, they would enter into a contract with the Lake City *ATR* voucher program which entitles them to receive a case manager, who would assist the offender as long as necessary to complete the program. In the first meeting between the offender and the case manager, a Single Coordinated Care Plan (SCCP) would be developed.

A Single Coordinated Care Plan (SCCP) was a strength based care plan individualized for each offender. The care plan was utilized to document: (i) the offender's vision for recovery, (ii) prioritize offender needs, and (iii) identify alternatives that could be used to meet the needs of the offender. The SCCP was updated on a monthly basis (at least once every two months) when the offender, case manager, probation/parole agent, treatment provider, and other ancillary service providers meet. This allowed for practitioners from a variety of social service and government agencies to formally collaborate to assist the offender in their reintegration in the Lake City community.

In addition to hearing from formal supports of the offender, the *ATR* program also focused on the informal supports of the offender. Therefore, within this monthly Recovery Support Team Meeting (RST), an offender would be expected to invite family, friends, or anyone who were able to assist in their recovery and transition to the community. These monthly meetings allowed for information to be shared by different government, non-government and family/friends to understand an offender's issues via a holistic approach. During these RST meetings, several issues would be discussed, which could include: drug testing, housing, employment, treatment, family problems and legal issues. Based on case file review, it was possible to identify what occurred during these meetings, which needs were met and how, as well as what caused offenders to be successful or unsuccessful in the program.

Reviewing case files in their entirety allowed the researcher to make systematic determinations of offenders within the *ATR* program. Other documentation within each offender case file included: (i) case manager notes on individual and RST meetings, (ii) documentation of voucher services such as employment, training, housing and treatment, (iii) paperwork regarding the abstinence of the offender throughout the program, criminal activity, reasons for an offender's discharge from the program and follow-up information.

Finally, the researcher developed a comprehensive database to identify significant variables, and responses that could be coded. Once coding was completed from the case file reviews, a Microsoft Excel database (which included names and birthdates of offenders participating in the *ATR* program) was developed. Upon development of this database, the researcher gained access to Lake City's State Court database. By utilizing this database system, it allowed the researcher access to public records of the circuit courts of the *ATR* site to measure recidivism (using offender names and birthdates). This court database case management system is currently used by court staff in the counties where the case files are located. Each court record was a summary of all public records under the Lake City's open records law.

A study can be considered valid if its measures actually measure what they claim to, and if there are no logical errors in drawing conclusions from the data. Each type of validity was concerned with the threats and/or biases which would undermine the meaningfulness of research (Maxfield and Babbie, 2006).

Internal Validity

Internal validity can be explained as defending against the sources of bias which can arise within the research design. This can have an effect on the causation process being studied by introducing covert variables. When there is lack of internal validity, variables can be found responsible for part or all of the observed effect on the dependent variable.

To increase the internal validity of the study, the researcher utilized a triangulation of sources in both the pretest and posttest phase to identify program effectiveness (success of offenders) and recidivism (reduction of criminal activity). Triangulation is the process of collecting information from a diverse range of individuals and settings, using a variety of methods (Patton, 1990). As Patton explained (1990:188), studies that utilized only one source of data had a higher risk of violating internal validity because they were more vulnerable to errors in the particular methodology of the study. It allowed the researcher to increase the quality and credibility of the research findings.

External Validity

External validity is the possible bias in the process of generalizing conclusions from a sample to a population, to other subject populations, to other settings, and/or to other time periods (Maxfield and Babbie, 2006). Can the findings of Lake City be replicated and perhaps generalized to other *ATR* jurisdictions? What is the uniqueness of this particular study? Naturally, when a sample of observations is not randomized, the likelihood of external validity is low, as in the case of convenience samples.

The researcher acknowledges that this program evaluation was unique in that it incorporated a variety of government agencies and social services in the assistance of offenders reentering into Lake City. Therefore, many of the findings may not be generalizable to other jurisdictions. This does not mean that the study is flawed, but rather unique which offers more insight on (i) an offender's reentry into the community and (ii) a systems approach to reentry. In addition to exploring these offenders, the study also hopes to shed light on the black box of offender recidivism.

Reliability

Reliability is the consistency of a set of measurements or measuring instrument. Therefore, reliability does not imply validity. A reliable measurement is when the study is able to measure the variables consistently. Reliability is the extent to which the measurements of a study remain consistent over repeated tests of the same subject under identical conditions (Maxfield and Babbie, 2006). An experiment is reliable if it yields consistent results of the same measure. It is unreliable if repeated measurements give different results.

The proposal developed by Lake City did not adequately address the evaluation designs of the program. Therefore, many of the variables developed were constructed by the researcher. Further evaluation of this Lake City program, in addition to other evaluations across the country will shed more insight on the consistency of the conceptualization and operationalization of the variables utilized in this study.

Limitations

There are several general limitations the researcher wishes to address based on the validity and reliability of the study. First, the study addresses the generalizability of the Lake City *ATR* program to other faith based research programming being conducted. Due to the nature of the SAMHSA grants, each *ATR* program outlined different grantee proposals. Therefore, no *Access To Recovery* program site had been implemented using the same method. Subsequently, each site was unique, each system was unique, and the implementation and development of the programming was unique. As explained above, the researcher felt that such an *ATR* study was important enough to measure, even though the results and analysis may not be generalizable to other jurisdictions. Therefore, it should be noted that this study was a case study of one *ATR* program that was funded by SAMHSA.

Second, the study evaluated the Lake City program, based the proposal Lake City submitted to SAMHSA. The researcher utilized the first year of three years of offender information to generate the results (which can be seen in Chapter IV). This was preliminary data in that it only accounts for the first year of the grantee's operation. It also accounts for offender's first opportunity to be enrolled in the *ATR* program. The data used in the analysis did not measure a second or third opportunity that an offender was given in the program.

Third, the researcher would have chosen to use a more formidable experimental design with an experimental and control group. However, due to restraints and restrictions placed on the researcher by the *ATR*'s Department of Corrections (DOC), the researcher was unable to locate a comparison or control group that would have been a true experimental design. This study was severely hindered by the DOC failure to allow the researcher access to public information databases. However, the data reported in this study could be utilized to measure the outcomes of offenders who participated in the program.

Fourth, the researcher would have completed a more thorough evaluation of the process indicators of the study to identify what was working, what was not working, and what was promising within the *ATR* program. However, the researcher felt that limiting the scope of the project was necessary for both the brevity and clarity of a dissertation.

Further research and analysis should be completed before trying to explain the true variance of whether the program can be determined as an overall success or failure. The one group one shot experimental design is a common but limited design in both social science and correctional reentry evaluations on recidivism. Therefore, it is subject to similar threats to validity and reliability as other studies not using a treatment component.

RESEARCH MODELS

As explained in Chapter I, many scholars have argued that it is difficult to evaluate the effectiveness of a reentry program simply on the merits on whether it reduces offender's likelihood of committing criminal activity. This suggests the need for two complex research questions. First, Did the Lake City *ATR* alcohol and other drug abuse treatment program assist offenders reenter into their communities? Were offenders able to abstain from usage? Furthermore, were there empirically based factors that were able to predict who might be more successful in the *ATR* program? Did religious based programming have any effect on abstinence or recidivism? Second, Did the Lake City *ATR* program reduce offender recidivism?

Research Model I

The first research question explores the complexity and the black box of the success of offenders within the Lake City *ATR* program. Success was based and measured on two dependent variables. The first dependent variable measured whether each participant abstained from any alcohol and/or other drug usage. The primary purpose of the Lake City *ATR* program, as explained previously in chapters I and II, was to reduce offender's dependency on AODA. The second dependent variable used to gauge the effectiveness of the AODA component was whether the offender was successful in their completion of their client chosen treatment program.

The Lake City proposal states that there would be two basic criteria that could be utilized to measure the effectiveness of the program. Quoting directly from the initial proposal to SAMHSA, Lake City's *ATR* successful participants would require "four consecutive clean urine drops and majority of treatment plan goals met" (Lake City, 2003: 27).

Upon examining Lake City's *ATR* case files and interviewing case managers and administrators, it was clear that there was no accurate data collected to determine whether an offender had four consecutive clean urine drops. The *ATR* site administrators attempted to measure this based on monthly offender self report data, which was simply inadequate for the purpose of this study. Therefore, in an effort to conceptualize abstinence, this study utilized probation/ parole officer case files to systematically determine whether an offender had used alcohol and/or other drugs while completing their treatment. Within each offender's probation/ parole file were measurements of urinalysis testing (which is mandated by the State's department of corrections). Unfortunately, the researcher was unable to use AODA treatment agency files because many offenders were simply not drug tested and/or it was not done in a systematic way. Therefore, the researcher would define abstinence as an offender who did not use alcohol and/or other drugs through the duration of the programming. These offenders would be considered unsuccessful participants in the program.

Although the *ATR* program expected abstinence from their participants, the implementation allowed for offenders to potentially and repeatedly use AODA and remain in the program. A review of the *ATR* case manager, probation/ parole officer and treatment facility case files accurately provided this documentation. As indicated in AODA research, drug abusers are likely to make poor decisions and relapse (and many in the treatment field feel this is simply a product of detoxification). Therefore, the researcher added a second variable, whether the offender may/ may not have used AODA and still completed the program's goals based on a single coordinated care plan (developed by offenders, case managers, probation/parole agents, treatment specialists, and other Recovery Support Team [RST] invitees).

Once an offender's *ATR* case file was closed, case managers were expected to complete and code the offender's discharge form. On this form, the case manager identified why the offender was being discharged from the program. Although this variable could be based solely on case manager discretion, all documentation for government and non-government agencies were used to make a formal determination (rather than simply suggesting this could be a result of the discretion of the case manager; who may have a conflict of interest).

There were also a vast number of independent variables of interest the author was interested in learning about when exploring the complexities of the Lake City *ATR* program. Scholars argue that there are many outcomes that reentry programs strive to improve upon, and these are virtually never measured in traditional recidivism outcome evaluations (Petersilia, 2004b; Visher *et al.*, 2004). In an effort to explain this black box of reintegration, the author was curious of several factors known to increase or decrease an offender's success in reducing their AODA or recidivism.

Assessment and Referral

Clinical studies have identified two indices that can assist in the diagnosing of alcohol and other drug abuse. The author chose to examine whether these two indices (the Addiction Severity Index (ASI) score, American Society of Addiction Medicine Second Edition - Revised of Patient Placement Criteria (ASAM PPC-2R) score) would have an effect on the dependent variables. The researcher stipulates that the more barriers that an offender faces, based on the ASI and ASAM components, the less likely the offender would complete the program successfully.

Alcohol and Other Drug Abuse (AODA)

In addition to being involved in the *ATR* AODA program, and the ancillary services that may be provided, the author was also interested in the variability in the type of treatment an offender was able to receive (residential, inpatient or outpatient), the length of time (in months) an offender spent in treatment and the type of drug and/or polymer usage. Would these be significant factors in explaining which offenders are more or less likely to complete their ATR program successfully and/or reduce offender recidivism?

Faith based Treatment

Perhaps the most important question revolved around the third foundation for the need of the *ATR* grant – the efficacy of religious based treatment programming. As the literature on AODA treatment suggests, many people reduce their consumption of alcohol or drugs because of their faith and belief in a higher power to assist them in their life decisions. Therefore, the researcher tests and explores this particular variable (whether an offender received a faith based AODA treatment provider). If an offender received a faith based community provider, would the offender be more successful in treatment? Would the offender be less likely to commit criminal activity?

Case Management and Support Systems

Based on the individualized treatment philosophy of the Lake City *ATR* program, it was necessary to control for the discretion within case management. Similar to probation/parole officers, social service case managers handle each offender differently. Case management has the ability to change the dynamic of an offender's treatment throughout their participation in the program. Their discretion and individual attention to a holistic approach to reintegration can provide more insight in the black box of recidivism. Some case managers may be more stringent and duty bound by the rules of the program, while other case managers may favor a less micro managing approach with the offenders they worked with. The researcher would argue that due to the individual nature of the programming that case managers were very important to an offender's successful discharge in the program.

Studies have found that formal (case managers, probation/parole agents, law enforcement, court and correctional officials) and informal relationships can have an effect on an offender's lifestyle and behavior. Therefore, would case managers have a significant effect on success or failure (simply due to their discretion within the *ATR* program)? And furthermore, would the inclusion of friends and family in the re-integrative process reduce AODA and recidivism? Would this remain consistent with other studies?

Housing and Shelter

Most offenders end up living with the same family and/or friends they had before being incarcerated. Many offenders are left with fewer options. Most correctional agencies three quarter and halfway houses are usually full in the fall and winter months, therefore many offenders find themselves living between shelters and on the streets. How many offenders received monetary or government assistance for housing and/or shelter? The researcher would argue that this may be a significant indicator in improving the quality of life of offenders, reducing their dependency on AODA and perhaps reducing their likelihood of recidivism.

Health Care

The vast majority of offenders released from prison do not have any form of medical insurance. Therefore, securing health care is a major concern for many released offenders. However, many corrections agencies lack any discharge planning and preparation to addressing the health care needs of offenders upon release. This makes continuity of care extremely difficult. This study will explore the health care services that some offenders received.

Mental Health

Inmates with mental illness are also increasingly being imprisoned and ultimately being released. Offenders who receive mental illness assistance may be more likely to desist from co-occurring AODA and be less likely to be engaged in criminal behaviors that eventually lead to arrest and conviction.

Employment and Vocational Training

When many offenders leave jail and/or prison, they may find themselves out of work. Once released, probation/ parole officers will be more likely than not to expect offenders to find a job and subsequently accumulate some money, and eventually find their own residence. Finding a job is often the most serious concern among offenders, who have few job skills and little work history. Their age at release, their lack of employment at time of arrest, and their history of substance abuse problems make it difficult to find a good job. Therefore, many released inmates quickly return to substance abuse and/or criminal activity. There are also questions surrounding transportation, clothing, hygiene and ancillary services that most studies to not measure. This study will look to advance our knowledge as to whether assisting offenders in these services has an effect on AODA and recidivism.

Education

Will the availability of educational attainment programs (e.g. completing high school *degree*, GED) have any effect on an offender's success in the *ATR* program or their recidivism?

In addition to these variables were other variables that could be controlled for to determine who might be the most successful in Lake City's *ATR* program. So in addition to the questions above, the author explored the differences in offender demographics (sex, age, race, ethnicity, marital status, religion, education, training and employment). However, to find causation, multivariate logistic regression and survival analysis were performed on the two dependent models discussed below to potentially answer which factors would be significant in determining success in Lake City's *Access To Recovery* program.

Research Model II

As explained in the literature review, the second research question of this study explores whether the Lake City *ATR* program reduced offender recidivism. Due to the complexity and multi-dimensionality of the recidivism, more in-depth discussion is needed to generate an understanding of how recidivism will be measured, both conceptually and operationally.

The researcher conceptualized recidivism using five measurements: (i) one or more documented incidences of probation/ parole technical violations; (ii) a warrant for non-compliance of an offender's terms of probation/ parole (which could include absconding from custody); (iii) arrest of a new crime; (iv) conviction of a new crime; and (v) incarceration of an offender to jail and/or prison. Each of the five measurements was taken at two month intervals while offenders were completing the Lake City *ATR* treatment program. This was done for the specific intent of using interval based statistical analysis. The following criteria were operationalized below.

For the purposes of this study, the researcher only counted the primary episode of an offender's treatment within the *ATR* program. If at any time the offender (i) absconded from the program (a two week period in which they have no contact with probation/ parole or case management); (ii) had a warrant against him/ her; or (iii) was incarcerated for over two weeks, their case was closed.

Probation/Parole Technical Violations

This was any action or behavior which an offender (knowingly or unknowingly) violated the terms of their probation and/or parole as adjudicated by a judge within the state. These violations were documented by the probation/ parole agent and subsequently signed by the offender. For the purposes of this research, there were two methods to measure these violations: (i) the offender reported the violation to the case worker and the information was documented in case notes or (ii) during monthly meetings between the case worker, probation/parole officer and offender, a violation occurred and was documented in the case notes. If the offender received a violation, they would still be eligible for the program. If the violation was one in which further incarceration was needed, the probation/parole agent or their supervisor could bring charges against the offender for violating their terms of probation/ parole. Under the terms of their supervision, offenders could be incarcerated either in jail or prison for an undisclosed amount of time. If this occurred, it was possible that an offender could re-apply to the program, but they would not have been included in the study's analysis.

Warrant for Arrest

A warrant could have been issued by the jurisdiction so that a preventative arrest could be made by law enforcement and/or probation/parole officers. Such a warrant was needed when the offender had a probation/parole violation, was a suspect in a current or previous civil or criminal case, and/or wanted by the Department of Corrections for absconding from custody. If a warrant was granted by a judge, the offender would no longer be eligible for the program and would have to re-apply.

Arrest

This variable was defined as the arrest of an offender by the police within the jurisdiction. This would not necessarily mean that charges had been laid against the offender for a new or previous criminal activity. The researcher operationalized arrest based on the self reporting of the offender to the probation/ parole agent in the jurisdiction (which was required based on their conditions of probation or parole). This information was further passed along to case management personnel within the *ATR* program for documentation. Therefore, re-arrest was measured by the information relayed from the offender to the probation/ parole officer and/or case manager. If an offender was arrested, they were still eligible for the *ATR* program.

Conviction
This variable would be defined when/ if an offender was charged and convicted of a new crime within the jurisdiction. The researcher operationalized conviction by utilizing the Lake City's circuit court database. By utilizing this database system, it allowed the researcher access to certain public records of the circuit courts of the

ATR site
The information that was displayed within the database was an exact copy of the case information entered into the case management system. The court record summaries were all public records under the Lake City's open records law. Despite a new conviction, an offender could still be eligible for the *ATR* program.

Incarceration
There were several methods for which an offender could have been re-incarcerated. First, if an offender was found guilty of violating the terms of their probation or parole they could be sent back to jail and/or prison (to complete some or all of their sentence) as required by the *ATR* site's truth in sentencing legislation. Second, an offender could be processed through the Lake City court system and found guilty of a civil or criminal matter and punished in jail and/or prison. The researcher operationalized incarceration by utilizing the same Lake City circuit court database. By utilizing this database system, it allowed the researcher access to certain public records of the circuit courts of the *ATR* site. Once an offender was re-incarcerated, they were dismissed from the program. If offender was released, they would be eligible to reapply for the program (but not eligible for this study).

Previous criminal record

The researcher was also very interested in two independent variables – an offender's lifetime criminal record and whether the offender was convicted of a violent or non-violent offense. Previous criminality may have a significant effect on understanding an offender's propensity to use AODA and/or recidivate.

CHAPTER 4:

Study Results and Findings

This chapter presents the analysis and results of the current study in Lake City. The first section of this chapter will explain the basic and aggregate findings relative to the Lake City participants of the sample. The second section of the chapter will explore what has been coined as the black box of offender reintegration, with a particular focus on the efficacy of the Lake City *Access To Recovery* (*ATR*) alcohol and other drug abuse (AODA) treatment programming and ancillary services. The third section will examine the recidivism behavior of the offenders participating in the program. Within the second and third sections, the author will utilize multivariate analysis for further exploration to identify causal factors/ variable that can assist us in learning about reintegration programming and its impact on recidivism.

PROFILE OF LAKE CITY PARTICIPANTS

Based on case file reviews of the *ATR* program, approximately 456 offenders had engaged in the program between the period of May, 2005 and June, 2006. However, due to the lack of database implementation by Lake City administration, it was necessary to complete a thorough examination of each case file of every offender who participated in the program. Upon examination of the case files, 22 case files were incomplete or could not be validated for analysis. Of the 456 offenders who enrolled in the *ATR* program, 13 offenders received a second opportunity at the *ATR* program and 9 offender files were simply inaccurate or invalidated due to a number of factors such as an unreliable name, identification, birth date and/or screening documentation. Therefore, the database utilized from case file review accounts for 434 of the 456 offender case files. This accounts for 95% of all offenders who entered into the Lake City program within its first year of grant funding by Substance Abuse and Mental Health Services Administration (SAMHSA). Each of these demographic variables can also be viewed in Table 1

The general profile of a Lake City *ATR* participant was a younger Black male between 22 and 28. The national profile of returning prisoners has changed in ways that pose new challenges to successful reentry. However, the basic demographics have not changed significantly over the past twenty years.

Table 1 – Profile of Lake City Participants

Variables	Sample n	Percent	Mean	Median	Std. Deviation
Sex			.29	.00	.45
Male	307	70.7			
Female	127	29.3			
Age category			34.96	35.00	9.52
18-21	25	5.8			
22-28	117	27.0			
29-35	78	18.0			
36-42	104	24.0			
43-49	82	18.9			
Over 49	28	6.5			
Race			.75	1.00	.60
White	133	30.6			
Black	289	66.6			
Native	7	1.5			
Pacific	2	.5			
Other	3	.7			
Ethnicity			.07	.00	.26
Hispanic	31	7.1			
Non Hispanic	403	92.9			
Marital			.17	.00	..37
Single	361	83.2			
Married	73	16.8			

Sex

Based on current Bureau of Justice Statistics research, the parole population was mostly male (88%), although the number of incarcerated females had risen steadily over the past decade (Glaze and Bonczar, 2006). Therefore, it was expected that males were more representative of the study sample, as they were far more likely to be incarcerated than women. However, men accounted for 71% of all offenders that enrolled in the program. Consequently, this study oversampled women that returning from prison.

Although women only make up about twelve percent of inmates, the number of women in prison has risen by 336% since 1980, compared to a 189% rise for men (Belenko and Peugh, 2005). In this study, women accounted for nearly one-third (29%) of all participants in the *ATR* program than those represented in national statistics (12%). So this study may be better in explaining the disparities between male and female reintegration and recidivism. Although substance involved women and men in prison share some of the same treatment needs, the manifestations and severity of these needs differ, particularly related to mental and physical health, vocational training, employment, family issues, prenatal and postnatal care, risk of HIV and other infectious diseases, and treatment design (Belenko and Peugh, 2005). Mental health problems are more likely and distinct for drug involved female than male inmates.

Women who abuse substances often suffer more intense emotional distress, psychosomatic symptoms, depression, and self-esteem problems than males. Parental responsibility can also undermine a woman's ability to participate in post release treatment and other services. Finally, there has been little use of discharge planning or continuity of care for female inmates, contributing to high rates of recidivism and relapse (Hammett *et al.*, 1998).

Age

The national median age of offenders returning to the community was thirty four in 2004 (Glaze and Bonczar, 2007).

Of all offenders enrolled in the Lake City treatment program, 27% of all offenders were between the ages of 22 and 28 with the median age being 35; this is remarkably close to that of the national average. Furthermore, other age groups were well represented: 6% of offenders were between the ages of 18 and 21; 18% of offenders were between 29 and 35; 24% between 36 and 42; 19% between 43 and 49; and 7% over the age of 50. There are very few studies that are able to locate a link between age and criminal desistence. Sampson and Laub's (2001) work on life-course transitions and desistence has illustrated the importance of life events on criminal offending. Many offenders continue to persist in a variety of crimes despite their age. Sampson and Laub identify these offenders who either desist or persist in criminal activity as having zigzag criminal careers, which were difficult to forecast (Laub and Sampson, 2003).

Age has also been shown to have a positive relationship with the successful completion of probation (Sims and Jones, 1997). Clarke *et al.* (1988) found that the younger age of probationers was significantly related to recidivism rates among a sample of North Carolina felony probationers. Benedict and Huff-Corzine (1997) discovered that older probationers committed more serious offenses than did their younger counterparts and therefore were more likely to be rearrested for a felony. However, these are only a handful of studies of hundreds of which could not find significance of age in desistence in criminal activity (Laub and Sampson, 2001).

Race and Ethnicity

Studies indicate that more than half (55%) the returning offenders in 1998 were white, whereas 44% were black. Hispanics were also found to be overrepresented at 21% of all those offenders on parole in 1998 (Bonczar and Glaze, 1999:147). Black males had a 29% chance of being incarcerated at least once in his lifetime, six times higher than that for white males. In fact, the Bureau of Justice Statistics estimated that nine percent of black males in their late 20s and three percent of Hispanic males in their late 20s were in prison at the end of 1999

(Beck, 2000:14). Looked at differently, more than one-third of black male high school dropouts were in prison or jail in the late 1990s; a higher percentage of this group were imprisoned than employed (Western and Pettit, 2000:11).

As explained previously, Black males were the most likely demographic group to be represented in the study sample. Black offenders accounted for 67% or two-thirds of all offenders who enrolled in the *ATR* program. White offenders consisted of 31% of offenders. When participants responded to their ethnicity, only a small percentage reported being Native Americans (2%) and Asian Americans (.5%). Therefore, it would be difficult to make any generalizations of these two demographic groups simply because their lack of representation in the study. Approximately 7% of all participants in the *ATR* program identified themselves as Hispanic/Latino (a smaller representative sample than was expected).

Marital Status

Hirschi's (1969) social bonding theory would offer the premise that offenders who were married and were being supervised within the criminal justice system would be less likely to recidivate. A significant amount of empirical research has found that marital status has predictive power in explaining offender recidivism (Petersilia, 1985; Sims and Jones, 1997). Clarke *et al.* (1988) concluded that being divorced or separated compared to offenders that had never been married was marginally significant in probation success or failure. Petersilia (1999) suggests that the presence of children in the home had a positive influence on probation success. When Lake City *ATR* participants were asked whether their marital status, a significant majority (83%) reported being single, while only 17% reported being married.

The Black Box

Exploring the black box of offender reintegration will require the author to explain and assist the reader in identifying the purposes of the Lake City *ATR* program from assessment and referral for alcohol and other drug abuse (AODA) to the ancillary services that offenders may have received. Furthermore, this section will explore whether these variables and other demographic variables (using multivariate analysis) impacted an offender's success within the Lake City *Access To Recovery* program.

Assessment and Referral

Assessment and referral is integral to understanding the profile of the offenders in the Lake City jurisdiction. Based on the Addiction Severity Index (ASI), a majority of offenders were found to need moderate to considerable treatment and should be placed in intensive inpatient and outpatient treatment (based on aggregate ASAM level of care scoring). Subsequently 83% of the offenders in the sample were recommended for intensive inpatient and outpatient treatment. However, there was a disparity in the numbers of offenders needing intensive treatment (51%) and those that received it (30%). Based on interviewees, it was prevalent that *ATR* participants were more likely to use crack/cocaine (46%) and be involved in multiple/ polymer drug abuse (86%) to control the highs and lows of their addiction.

Despite the moderate to considerable treatment most offenders needed, an astonishing 91% of offenders engaged in some form of immediate treatment within the first month of the *ATR* program. Although these numbers decreased as months followed, the median length of time offenders spent in treatment was nearly four and a half months. Nearly half, 47% of offenders were found to remain sober and abstinent throughout their entire treatment modality.

Prior to being released from prison, a presentation of the *ATR* program was made by *ATR* clinical screeners to educate offenders, who were interested in the treatment modalities and eligibility requirements of the *ATR* program. Upon completion of the presentation, offenders could choose to enter into the program. As explained in previous chapters, due to the rewards of the program, the researcher was unable to implement an experimental model. Therefore, there was no control group subsample as a large percentage, over 95% of the entire offender population returning to Lake City, voluntarily wanted access to the program's rewards.

Once released from jail and/or prison, offenders were immediately prescreened for the Lake City *ATR* treatment program within a 48-hour period. Before being given a case manager, clinical screeners were trained and recruited to proctor two indices. The first, the Addiction Severity Index (ASI), is the most widely used alcohol and drug assessment tool in the evaluation of substance abuse treatment. The ASI has been established as the standard assessment tool for alcohol and other addictions (Leonard *et al.,* 2000).

The ASI is an interview that assesses the history, frequency, and consequences of alcohol and drug use, as well as five additional domains that are commonly associated with drug use: medical, employment, legal, social/family, and psychological functioning. The higher the score on the ASI indicates a greater need for treatment in each of these areas. Once a screener determines ASI scores, the scores can be used to profile an offender's problem areas and plan a course of effective, long term treatment (with the assistance of a case manager).

Based on the study sample, when the ASI was administered, offenders were found to have needed assistance for: medical (45%), employment (98%), alcohol (66%), drugs (78%), legal (66%), family (59%), and psychological/ mental health assistance (59%). Each offender's individual ASI scores were further aggregated so that each offender would have a scaled measurement for all seven variables determining their risk and/or need based on ASI assessments. The results of the data were as follows.

Based on ASI assessments, only three offenders (less than 1%) were diagnosed with no addiction severity with an index score less than .25 out of a potential 7 scored value. Each domain was measured using four indicators: (i) no addiction severity, (ii) some severity with moderate treatment needed, (ii) considerable treatment is needed, and (iv) extreme severity with intensive treatment and/or hospitalization required. Each domain was aggregated from its original range from 0 to 1. Therefore, once aggregated, the ASI index score could range between 0 and 7. Of the scaled index of a potential score of 7, a majority of offenders (52%) reported an index score less than 2; where some moderate treatment may be needed. Another 46% of offenders responded to need considerable treatment; having been diagnosed between a score of 2 and 4 out of a potential score of 7. A final 1% reported having a score between 4 and 4.75. There were no offenders within the sample that received a score about 4.75 out of a possible 7.

The ASAM 2nd Edition of the Revised of Patient Placement Criteria (ASAM PPC-2R), was the second well known assessment tool that the Lake City *ATR* program used for placement and continued stay of offenders with substance abuse. The ASAM was also used because of its strength in determining the scope of co-occurring mental and substance-related disorders (or dual diagnosis). The ASAM outlines five broad levels of care for each type of offender: early intervention, outpatient, intensive outpatient/ day treatment, residential, and medical managed intensive inpatient treatment. Within these broad levels of service are criteria based on six dimensions: acute intoxication/ withdrawal potential; biomedical conditions and complications; emotional, behavioral or cognitive conditions and complications; readiness to change; relapse, continued use or continued problem potential; and recovery environment.

Based on the ASAM instrument, almost all offenders reported some broad levels of service assistance. Based on the six dimensions of the ASAM, offenders reported: a withdrawal potential (18%), biomedical conditions (49%), emotional/ behavioral/cognitive complications (63%), readiness to change (88%), potential to relapse (93%), and a poor recovery environment (80%). Each dimension was aggregated from its original range from 0 to 4. Once aggregated, ASAM measurements were scored between 0 and a potential 24 index.

Upon further aggregation of the ASAM dimensions, only one offender (representing .2% of the sample) fell within the upper range of 18 to 24, which would require medically managed intensive residential treatment. The remainder of offenders would need lesser treatment levels of care. Approximately 37% of all offenders were diagnosed with a need for early intervention, which would require some outpatient treatment. A majority of offenders (51%) were diagnosed with a need for intensive outpatient treatment. The remainder of offenders (6%) has been diagnosed with a need for low, medium, or high intensity residential treatment level of care.

Based on screener assessments and offender client choice of treatment options, approximately 53% of offenders entered into outpatient treatment, 30% entered into intensive outpatient treatment, and 17% of offenders entered into residential treatment (Table 2). The data on level of care suggests that more offenders were placed into residential treatment than should have been necessary. However, it should be noted that if offenders were placed into residential treatment, they would be given a traditional duration of three months in which they could live rent free while engaging in treatment. Therefore, many offenders may have taken advantage of this opportunity.

Table 2 – Participant Assessment and Referral

Variable	Sample n	Percent	Mean	Median	Std. Deviation
ASI			2.03	.10	.24
Low	228	52.5			
Medium	200	46.1			
High	6	1.4			
ASAM			8.03	8.00	3.58
Low	199	45.9			
Medium	223	51.4			
High	12	2.8			
Level of Care			1.64	1.00	.75
Outpatient	231	53.2			
Inpatient	130	30.0			
Residential	73	16.8			

As a requirement of the *ATR* program, offenders were expected to self report an alcohol or drug abuse problem. Once offenders had done so, they proceed from the initial interview to a more comprehensive screening process. This was during the screening process, where each offender was asked a variety of questions to ensure they qualify *ATR* voucher programming. It was during this self report process within the initial interview that offenders reported having used multiple drugs during their abuse, and that crack/ cocaine was the drug of most concern for abuse.

Nearly half of all offenders (46%) reported abusing crack/ cocaine the most of any other drugs. Other offenders suggested that cannabis (26%), alcohol (19%), heroin (7%), and opiates (2%) were also of concern. However, 86% of offenders reported having used multiple drugs during their usage or binges. Therefore, it should be expected that offenders are trying to creatively manage the highs and lows of drug use by only using various types of drugs in combination.

Duration of Treatment

As the literature review explains, many AODA treatment programs find that treatment is very personal and dependent on the rapport of the facilitator-offender relationship that would hopefully be offset by the Lake City *ATR* client choice mandate. Therefore, there would be an expectation that offenders would create more meaningful relationships with their treatment advisors. Approximately 10% of all offenders either chose or removed from the *ATR* program within the first month. Subsequently, a surprising 90% of offenders chose to complete at least some AODA treatment within their first month of treatment. Within the first two months, 72% of offenders remained in some form of AODA treatment. After 4 months, there was still a surprising majority (54%) of offenders who remained in treatment. The median time in which offenders remained in the *ATR* program was approximately four and a half months. By the end of the fourth month, many offenders began to withdraw from the program, were terminated due to rule violations, and/or absconded from treatment, ending their participation in the program. After the sixth month of treatment, only 29% of offenders were in either mandated or voluntary treatment.

AODA Abstinence

As explained in chapters above, the researcher chose to examine two variables to determine whether the program was successful in (i) offender's abstaining from alcohol and other drug abuse, and (ii) whether offenders participating in the *ATR* met their program goals (which will be explained in the next section of the chapter). This operation of success was derived from the grant proposal made to SAMHSA. Four consecutive clean urine samples were expected to be conducted on offenders. However, there was no systematic documentation to test this success measurement. Therefore, the offender's case file (offender self report data, urinalysis from probation/ parole, urinalysis from treatment providers) were used to determine each offender's success or failure.

Based on descriptive statistics, statistics indicate that approximately half or 47% of all offenders participating in the *ATR* program remained abstinent throughout the program. This indicates that a small majority, 53% of offenders relapsed into alcohol and drug abuse. After the first two months of AODA treatment, approximately 42% of all offenders had either self reported AODA usage or failed a drug/ urinalysis test.

During the duration of treatment for those offenders who continued through *ATR* programming, findings indicate that offender AODA use was reduced significantly (Table 3). Controlling for an offender's time in treatment, AODA usage was reduced at each two month interval; 34% between months three and four, 21% between months five and six, 10% between months seven and eight, 6% between months nine and ten, 3% in months eleven and twelve. This statistic would indicate that through commitment, many offenders may have relapsed but decided to continue throughout the program.

Table 3 – Participant AODA Usage

Variables	Sample n	Percent	Mean	Median	Std. Deviation
Prevalent Drug			1.46	2.00	.95
C/Crack	200	46.1			
Heroin	31	7.1			
Marijuana	112	25.8			
Alcohol	84	19.4			
Other	7	1.7			
Polymer Drug			.86	1.00	.35
Multiple use	374	86.2			
No Multiple	60	13.8			
Duration			4.51	4.00	2.86
Less 2 mths	122	28.1			
3-4 mths	129	29.7			
5-6 mths	93	21.4			
7-8 mths	48	11.1			
9-10 mths	19	4.4			
Over 10mths	23	5.3			
Abstinence			.41	.00	.49
Once >	179	41.2			
No	255	58.8			
Faith-Based			.19	.00	.40
Requested	84	19.4			
Not requested	350	80.6			
Religion			1.88	1.00	1.86
Catholic	105	24.2			
Protestant	54	12.4			
Baptist	39	9.0			
Islamic	18	4.1			
Other	83	19.1			
No response	135	31.1			

Faith Based Treatment

Lake City's program initiative proposed by President Bush would provide people (including offenders) seeking drug and alcohol treatment with vouchers to pay for a range of appropriate community and faith based services (SAMHSA, 2006). Therefore, based on the data, few offenders took part in faith based programming. In fact, almost one-fifth (19%) of offenders were directly involved with faith based service providers that assisted in alcohol and other drug abuse treatment. It should be noted that this would not include offenders who engaged in voluntary programming on their own time (such as Twelve Step clubs or Alcoholic/Cocaine Anonymous). Interestingly enough, within the prescreening interviews, over two-thirds (69%) reported being religious. Most of offenders reported being Catholic (24%), of other religions (19%) and Protestant (12%). The remainder of offenders reported being Baptist (9%) and Muslim (4%).

However, these are not the only factors that contribute to success within a systems approach to offender reintegration. As explained in the literature review, offender reintegration within a systems approach targets each individual offender's areas of need or risk while completing some form of AODA/behavioral/ cognitive treatment. During the development of the single coordinated care plan (SCCP); case managers, probation/parole agents, treatment providers and an offender (and their informal support network) would agree upon the goals that the offender should expect to meet to be successful in the *ATR* program. In addition to completing AODA treatment, the author was very interested in understanding other resources offenders received, further exploring the factors that may or may not impact recidivism.

Case Management and Support Systems

Generally speaking, case managers are often used to supervise offenders within a coordinated systems approach. As a result of escalating case loads for probation/ parole agents, case managers are needed to supervise and monitor each offender based on their performance in the program.

Upon completion of an initial interview and screening instrumentation, offenders were immediately wait-listed for *ATR* treatment and services. The Lake City voucher program entitled each offender to an intensive supervisory case manager. Although each case manager was committed to assisting offenders' re-integration into Lake City, there were also high expectations of offenders if they received perceived resources and rewards for their behavior in AODA treatment. During the process of studying the program in Lake City for its first year of existence, nine case managers were asked to take on approximately 25 participants of the program based on the eligibility and program requirements. Over that period of time, 434 offenders (that could be validated by official data records) were studied.

It was the role of a Lake City *ATR* case manager to bring together all informal and formal support groups into the treatment single coordinated care plan (SCCP) process. Each case manager would work directly with the offender as long as necessary to complete the program. In the first meeting between the offender and the case manager, a SCCP would be developed which was considered a strength based care plan individualized for each offender. The care plan was utilized to document: (i) the offender's vision for recovery, (ii) prioritize offender needs, and (iii) identify alternatives that can be used to meet the needs of the offender. The SCCP was updated on a monthly basis (at least once every two months) when the offender, case manager, probation/parole agent, treatment provider, and other ancillary service providers would meet. All information was then placed in case files thereby allowing the researcher to locate specific areas of interest that were discussed in these meetings. This allowed for criminal justice practitioners to collaborate with variety of social service and non-government agencies to assist the offender in their reentry to their community.

In addition to hearing from formal supports of the offender, the *ATR* program also focused on the informal supports of the offender. Therefore, within these monthly recovery support team meetings (RST), an offender would be expected to invite family, friends, or anyone who was able to assist in their recovery and transition to the community. These monthly RST meetings allowed for information to be voiced about the offender; their strengths and weaknesses while participating in the program.

Based on all available data on monthly RST meetings, offenders were encouraged to invite people within their network of friends, family and acquaintances that could assist in their AODA treatment and/or reintegration into the community. Despite its emphasis in the *ATR* program proposal to SAMHSA, only 13% (57) of offenders' families, friends and/or acquaintances participated in the SCCP process. As an offender's treatment continued, and they progressed through the Lake City program, the likelihood of family or friend's involvement in SCCP diminished significantly; from 12% (54) in the first two months, 6% (25) in months three and four, 4% (16) in months five and six, 2% (8) in months seven and eight, to 1% (5) of offenders who still participated in the program in months nine through twelve.

The Lake City program, like other systems approaches to alcohol and other drug abuse (AODA) treatment programs was based on a holistic approach. This approach was designed to utilize an offender's informal social support system, rather than simply being forced by formal support mechanisms, such as police, courts and correctional personnel. Therefore, the *ATR* program was designed to incorporate families, children, friends and other non-government organizations (such as churches) to be involved in the rehabilitation of each offender. This individual-based holistic program has been found to be effective in correctional rehabilitation, while also reducing recidivism (Sherman *et al.,* 1997; Aos *et al.*, 2006).

With intensive case management/ supervision and the inclusion of informal supports for offenders, it was expected that offenders would progress with more ease in their reintegration into the community. It was assumed that during RST meetings, criminal justice and social service practitioners as well as informal supports (friends and family of the offender) would be present to assist the offender in their treatment and reentry issues. This could include issues with treatment efficacy and drug testing to the need for ancillary services, such as housing, employment, or transportation. All SCCP documentation was utilized for coding purposes. Additional documentation was available to validate any voucher services that an offender received. The study also utilized documentation regarding offender AODA abstinence throughout the program, their criminal activity, reasons for an offender's discharge from the program and potential follow-up information. Based on case file reviews, it was possible to identify what occurred in these meetings, which needs were met and how, as well as what caused offenders to be successful/ unsuccessful in the program.

Grant Assistance

Overall, offenders received a significant amount of resources. Only 31 of 434 offenders participating in the *ATR* program received no grant assistance (Table 4). This likely can be explained because these offenders absconded from the program and/or simply did not want/ need the resources. Although there was availability in resources, these resources were controlled by the discretion of *ATR* administrators, case managers, probation/ parole agents, and treatment providers. Although this program examined only outcome based measurements, the author finds it necessary to recommend that a process measurement (beyond the scope of this book) would be necessary to identify how these discretionary decisions impacted each offender and the resources they could receive.

Table 4 – Case Management and Grant Assistance

Variables	Sample n	Percent	Mean	Median	Std. Deviation
Case Management			1.00	1.00	.00
Received	434	100.0			
Not Received	0	0.0			
Information Support			.13	.00	.34
RST attend	57	13.1			
No attend	377	86.9			
Grant Assistance			1.00	1.00	.26
Received	403	92.9			
Not Received	31	7.1			

The author can say with certainty that the program opened the opportunities for offenders that Lake City was previously unable to provide. However, in RST meetings, case managers, probation/parole agents and treatment facilitators felt differently when asked to determine how successful offenders were in completing their single coordinated care plan (SCCP) goals.

Housing and Shelter

As explained in the literature review, many offenders leave prison without any housing plans. In many circumstances, a state's department of corrections system may have some placement for the offender for a short period of time (halfway or three-quarters house). However, due to the large numbers of offenders churning through the system and the lack of funding available for community based corrections (versus institutional corrections), many offenders could be neglected. The results of this study found that half or 50% of offenders who participated in the *ATR* program received some form of housing assistance based on a voucher program (Table 5). This housing could include: housing at a residential treatment facility, or rental assistance for their own or family dwelling (which could an apartment, short term stay hotel rooms, living with a friend/ roommate expenses, etc.). This voucher program was not associated with halfway/ three quarter housing operated by the state's Department of Corrections. What we do know was that when Department of Correction housing was calculated, approximately 83% of all offenders in the sample were given some form of housing. Other offenders lived with friends, family and/or resided in daily shelters.

Health Care

Many offenders released from prisons and/or jails are poor and unable to pay for health or medical insurance. Therefore, once released, these offenders become a burden on the social services systems. Of the 434 offenders enrolled in the *ATR* program, approximately 152, or 35% received funding which resulted in six to twelve months of free (no co-pay based) medical/ emergency care within the Lake City's State system (Table 5). This identifies a disturbing yet well understood statistic, that even when given the option of free health care, a majority (65%)

of offenders simply chose not to complete the required paperwork and/or did not see the need.

Table 5 – Participant Programming and Discharge

Variables	Sample n	Percent	Mean	Median	Std. Deviation
Housing			.50	1.00	.50
Received	218	50.2			
Not Received	216	48.8			
Health Care			.35	.00	.48
Received	152	35.0			
Not Received	282	65.0			
Mental Health			.09	.00	.29
Received	39	9.0			
Not Received	395	91.0			
Employ Assist			.43	.00	.50
Received	187	43.1			
Not Received	247	56.9			
Employment			—	—	—
Attained	178	41.0			
Not Attained	256	59.0			
Employment			—	—	—
Full time	64	35.9			
Part time	114	64.0			
Transportation			.68	1.00	.47
Received	297	68.4			
Not Received	137	31.6			
Clothing			.57	1.00	.50
Received	249	57.4			
Not Received	185	42.6			
Education			.19	.00	.35
Received	83	19.1			
Not Received	351	80.9			
ProgramRemoval			2.42	2.00	1.45
Successful	73	16.8			
Rule violated	45	10.4			
Abscond	194	44.7			
Withdrew	35	8.1			
Incarcerated	101	21.7			

Mental Health

A significant percentage of offenders returning to their communities after lengthy incarcerations have both an alcohol and drug abuse problem and co-occurring mental illness. In jail and/or prison, offenders may not have quality treatment options. Offenders often received medication for their symptoms, which may or may not be addressing the underlying problem. The grant provided for mental health assistance in collaboration with the Lake City County's mental health clinic. Approximately 9% of all offenders within the *ATR* program were found to have utilized resources towards mental illness, which included a diagnosis through Lake City's mental health clinic, and given low cost ($2 generic prescription) medications (Table 5). This also included all referrals for offenders that were completed by probation/parole officers. Considering that the ASI clinical instrument diagnosed 59% of offenders with a moderate to considerate need and/or assistance with mental illness. This problem and/or barrier seemed to go untreated in the majority of cases where medications were used as solutions (likely because additional counseling was never covered by the *ATR* program).

Employment and Vocational Training

Of all offenders participating in the Lake City *ATR* program, approximately 43% received some form of employment assistance (Table 5). In addition to the usage of free government and non-government services, many offenders received vocational training for technical trades. Other services that were most prominently used were employment specialists to assist in interview coaching, as well as employment providers in which the ATR vouchers paid for an offender's immediate training for an occupation they would be guaranteed once the training was completed.

Were these programs effective? Based on case file reviews, nearly 20% of all offenders were successful in finding some employment during those initial two weeks after being released. However, using bi-variate analysis, it was found that there was an equal chance of receiving employment whether employment assistance was granted by the *ATR* site. At its height, as many as 41% of offenders received some form of paid job (whether it be part time [64%] or full time [36%]). As explained in Chapter 2, there are also other factors to consider rather than simply receiving employment assistance.

A majority of offenders are usually unable to find adequate transportation to and from their treatment appointments, probation/parole officer meetings, a job, or vocational training. This roadblock was alleviated through the *ATR* program. Approximately 68% of all offenders received some transportation assistance. This assistance usually took the form of a weekly bus pass. With community and faith based providers located throughout Lake City area, it was a necessary for a majority of offenders to receive a bus pass giving them the flexibility and guarantee that they could keep their obligations to the program. In select cases, offenders able to find employment were given an opportunity to reapply for their driver license. Twenty-three, or 5% of offenders were given the $45.00 re-application fee so that they may be more proactive in their employment and/or treatment strategy success.

Once released from jail and/or prison, many offenders had little to no resources at their disposal. In many cases, offenders left their prison cell with only the clothes they had when they were first admitted to prison. Therefore, many offenders had immediate personal hygiene and clothing needs. Based on immediate need, it was necessary to provide bundled food care packages as well as lists of free food and clothing service providers. However, service providers often lack the resources to provide for all people in social need. Therefore, case managers, in cooperation with supervisor oversight, would go shopping with offenders to purchase clothing and/or personal items for immediate use. This often resulted in the purchase of underwear, socks, jeans, and dress clothing for job interviews. Of 434 offenders, 249 offenders, or 58% received some form of clothing, hygiene, and/or personal care needs allowances. Although the scope of this program was simply outcome based, the author was actively involved in an offender's clothing benefit and was in both shock and awe at how significant a problem this has become. More research needs to be done on this black box of recidivism.

Education

Nationwide in 2004, the median grade level for offenders was grade eleven (Glaze and Bonczar, 2007). Once released from jail and/or prison into Lake City communities, offenders were given one week (and sometimes two weeks in some extreme cases) before beginning treatment programming. This time allowed them to find immediate employment, and/or begin completing their SCCP goals such as educational attainment. The findings of this study indicate that a limited percentage of offenders took advantage of educational assistance. Nearly one-fifth (19%) of all offenders who participated in the *ATR* program received educational or General Education Development (GED) assistance (Table 5). While services for completing a high school diploma were freely available, probation/parole agents often appeared reluctant that education would assist in immediate job attainment. Therefore, although this assistance was granted, the length and duration of these services rarely last more than one month. Of those 19% of offenders who received educational assistance, only 7% of those offenders attained some diploma based educational certificate, while 93% of offenders received a failing outcome.

Program Discharge

The first measurement of determining the effectiveness of the Lake City's *ATR* program was the discharge conditions/ outcomes reported within each offender's case file. Available data of the 434 offenders indicates that a majority of offenders were unsuccessful in completing the *ATR* programming and/or requirements. Approximately 45% of offenders absconded from the program (treatment provider, case manager or probation/ parole agent). After two weeks within abscond status, an offender was discharged unsuccessfully from the program. Other unsuccessful discharges resulted from withdrawing from the program (7%), rule violations (10%), and re-incarceration to a jail and/or prison system (23%). Subsequently, only 17% of offenders were successful in completing the majority of their SCCP goals developed within the recovery support team (RST) meetings (Table 5).

Based on the findings of frequencies and bi-variate analyses, the author would suggest that the *ATR* program was outstanding in their assessment and referral of resources to offenders. However, outcomes were likely impacted by the process of implementation of the program which critically limited the numbers of offenders who could receive resources (based on the author's experience). Of those offenders who received AODA treatment, a large minority (47%) were able to maintain abstinence while in the program. Due to the limitations of the study, it will be difficult to ascertain whether that sobriety continued following their successful dismissal from the program. Based on the second outcome measure, only 17% were considered successful in the completion of their SCCP goals. Should we be celebrating? Perhaps a more comprehensive exploration is needed to determine whether this program was effective in curbing recidivism.

RESEARCH MODEL I

The purpose of the Lake City *ATR* program, as explained in Chapters I and II, was to reduce offender's dependency on alcohol and other drug use (AODA), while also reducing the likelihood of criminal activity. The Lake City program's success was measured using two variables. The first model examined an offender's alcohol and drug abuse (AODA) abstinence while completing treatment. The second model identified factors that predicted the successful discharge from the program (completed by the offender's case manager).

To reduce the likelihood of multi-collinearity in the models, the author removed case outliers with over a 2.0 residual, which also had further residuals above seven. For the purposes of these following two research models, as many as three cases were removed for each of the regression analyses. As with logistical regression, it was necessary to determine the role of outliers in survival analysis. After examining the residuals and DfBetas, all outliers were removed. Once outlier cases were removed, there were 270 of the 434 cases that could be used for the seven logistic regression models.

Table 6; an offender's AODA Abstinence, illustrates the first of two dependent variables that the researcher has utilized to measure the effectiveness of the Lake City *ATR* program.

The variables within the model explain approximately 43% of offender abstinence while completing treatment programming. Within the first regression model, five variables: the ASAM referral, polymer drug use, the duration of treatment, the discretion within case managers, and those persons supporting an offender throughout their *ATR* programming were found to be influential (with a confidence level of 95% with the $p < .05$ being significantly different than zero).

The clinical ASAM instrument was found to be a predictor of AODA abstinence. The lower the risk and/or needs of an offender diagnosed by their ASAM score, the more likely they would remain abstinent from AODA. This is consistent with current literature that identifies the ASAM as an excellent assessment tools for offenders.

Offenders reported to having used multiple drugs in the past, were less likely to be abstinent in the Lake City program. The duration of time offenders remained in *ATR* treatment was also found to be a significant factor in predicting abstinence. The longer an offender remained in treatment, the more likely the offender would remain abstinent of AODA use. Although it is no surprise to many practitioners, this study found that offenders who remained in treatment for longer periods of time were more likely to be abstinent from alcohol and other drug use.

Case managers have the ability to influence the outcome of the offenders they work in close contact with. Case managers can encourage or discourage based on their particular ideology of treatment. Therefore, it should be no surprise that their discretion and rapport can influence the outcome of offender's AODA.

Table 6 – AODA Abstinence

Variables of Interest	B	S.E.	Sig.	
Sex (male)	0.44	0.44	.318	
Age	- 0.03	0.02	.164	
Race (Black)	- 0.33	0.45	.462	
Ethnicity(Hispanic)	0.07	0.81	.927	
Marital status (single)	0.76	0.49	.120	
ASI	- 0.25	0.29	.385	
ASAM	0.17	0.07	.013	*
Level of care	0.05	0.27	.861	
Prevalent drug (marijuana)	0.57	0.13	.256	
Polymer drug	- 1.71	0.73	.019	*
Duration	0.58	0.12	.000	*
Faith based treatment	0.11	0.48	.816	
Religion (Catholic)	0.42	0.64	.371	
Case management	1.19	0.09	.022	*
Informal support	3.32	0.61	.000	*
Housing	0.15	0.02	.942	
Health care	0.27	0.38	.716	
Mental health	0.22	0.50	.427	
Employment	0.19	0.08	.617	
Transportation	0.16	0.05	.129	
Clothing	0.37	0.91	.815	
Education	0.59	0.08	.439	
Years incarcerated	- 0.83	0.61	.171	
Prior convictions	0.03	0.06	.545	
Constant	- 0.07	1.49	.963	

Model -2 Log likelihood 190.101 Cox & Snell R Square .374
Nagelkerke R Square .427 Chi-square 203.125
Degrees of freedom 24 Model significance .003

The presence and influence of an offender's informal support system was found to be a significant predictor of an offender's abstinence while completing treatment. Family, friends and acquaintances who were present at offender Recovery Support Team (RST) meetings seemed to have a positive effect on an offender's abstinence. In addition, when the offender self-reported that they had trusted a family member more than any other person, these offenders were found to be more successful in remaining abstinent from AODA usage while in treatment.

The second research model also examines the efficacy of the Lake City program using a secondary indicator: an offender's successful discharge after completion of the program. Utilizing case manager's documentation, the researcher coded the possible success and/or failure of the offenders based on the program criteria for discharge: absconding, withdrawal, rule violation, or successfully completed the program.

The research model was effective in explaining 58% of an offender's successful discharge from the Lake City program. However, the model was more likely to predict the failure of an offender within the program than success in the program (96%; 60%; see Table 7). Five variables were found to be significant in explaining success within the *ATR* program: an offender's case manager, multiple (polymer) drug use, the time an offender remains in treatment, the presence of an informal support system during RST meetings, and employment assistance. As explained in a previous model, case managers are well networked with criminal justice and social service practitioners. Therefore, they hold some reputation and can have an effect (and based on this model), or a significant effect on whether they vouch for an offender's credibility or recommend that they be discharged unsuccessfully.

Offenders that reported multiple drug usage were found to be less likely to graduate successfully in the program. As offenders continue through the program, the data from the regression analysis suggests that the longer the offender remains in the program, the higher the likelihood they will graduate successfully.

The presence of an informal support system (family or friends) during an offender's Recovery Support Team (RST) meeting was also found to be an effective tool in measuring success.

Table 7 – Program Discharge

Variable of Interest	B	S.E.	Sig.	
Sex (male)	0.36	0.41	.378	
Age	0.00	0.02	.973	
Race (Black)	16.42	1.05	.752	
Ethnicity(Hispanic)	- 0.44	0.80	.584	
Marital status (single)	0.76	0.45	.088	
ASI	0.85	0.15	.254	
ASAM	0.29	0.52	.483	
Level of care	- 0.05	0.25	.858	
Prevalent drug (marijuana)	0.08	1.27	.243	
Polymer drug	- 1.48	0.69	.031	*
Duration	0.52	0.11	.000	*
Abstinence	2.31	0.61	.000	*
Faith based treatment	0.28	0.45	.544	
Religion (Catholic)	0.82	0.77	.094	
Case management	- 0.27	0.09	.002	*
Informal support	2.70	0.55	.000	*
Housing	- 0.35	0.49	.480	
Health care	0.80	1.51	.598	
Mental health	1.09	0.60	.069	
Employment	0.49	0.44	.043	*
Transportation	- 0.63	0.55	.251	
Clothing	- 1.63	1.06	.098	
Education	0.02	0.43	.962	
Years incarcerated	- 0.13	0.08	.101	
Prior convictions	- 0.01	0.06	.899	
Constant	- 2.25	6.23	.998	

Model -2 Log likelihood 208.458 Cox & Snell R Square .347
Nagelkerke R Square .582 Chi-square 184.767
Degrees of freedom 25 Model significance .000

This positive correlation would suggest that family and friends are keys in understanding correctional reintegration. In an effort to learn more about which programs would be the most effective in the *ATR* program, it seemed that finding employment was the only statistically significant factor that has an effect on an offender's success. Employment as a variable, not surprisingly, has also been found to be an important factor in recidivism as well.

Recidivism

In addition to examining the three general modalities of recidivism used in the 1983 and 1994 Bureau of Justice Statistics study (arrest, conviction and incarceration), the author also chose to examine technical violations and warrants for an offender's arrest. The author was also interested in whether an offender's previous criminal record would be a factor in their success in the *ATR* program and/or their recidivism during the first year of their release from prison.

Previous Criminal Record

In addition to examining demographic data, the researcher felt it was necessary to get baseline data on offenders' previous criminal records and incarceration. At the initial screening of potential participants in the *ATR* program, no offender's prior record could be used against their participation. Therefore, no offenders were discouraged from entering into the program. Screeners asked offenders to self report their previous criminal record and lifetime incarceration (see Table 8). Upon examining this data in case file reviews, the researcher validated this data by utilizing Lake City's State court database. By utilizing this database system, it allowed the researcher access to certain public records of the circuit courts of the *ATR* site to determine an offender's previous criminal record and length of incarceration (within the state).

When examining offender prior records and convictions, data from the Lake City State Court which was aggregated by the researcher found that 70% of all offenders participating in the treatment program had five or fewer convictions. Approximately 23% had between six and ten convictions, and 9.2% had 11 or more convictions. One offender was found to have been convicted of an astonishing nineteen offenses. The median number of convictions was five.

Table 8 – Recidivism

Variable	Sample n	Percent	Mean	Median	Std. Deviation
Priors			4.73	4.00	3.65
5 or less	300	69.1			
6-10	92	21.2			
11-15	36	0.8			
16 and over	6	0.1			
Yrs Incarcerated			4.22	4.00	2.86
1	78	18.0			
2	79	18.2			
3	55	12.7			
4	44	10.1			
5	39	9.0			
6	39	9.0			
7	23	5.3			
8	2	.5			
9 or more	75	17.3			
Tech Violation			.79	1.00	.41
No Violation	92	21.2			
Any Violation	342	78.8			
Warrant			.17	.00	.38
No Warrant	359	82.7			
Any Warrant	75	17.3			
Arrest			.30	.00	.46
No Arrest	304	70.0			
Any Arrest	130	30.0			
Conviction			.16	.00	.37
No Conviction	364	83.9			
Any Conviction	70	16.1			
Incarceration			.23	.00	.42
No Incarceration	333	76.7			
!> Incarceration	101	23.3			

The data collected from Lake City's State court database was then coded into the researcher's dataset for further analysis (to be explained later). Based on the data, approximately 6% of all offenders had spent less than six months in jail and/or prison. The median time that offenders were incarcerated, prior to their enrollment in the *ATR* program was approximately four years. A majority of offenders spent two years (12%), three years (17%), or four years (13%) incarcerated. As follows, offenders were still likely to spend a significant percentage of their lives in prison: five years (9%), six years (9%), seven years (5%) or eight years (5%). The largest percentage of all offenders (18%) spent nine or more years in prison.

In addition to examining participant's lifetime criminal record, recidivism was of significant interest. Recidivism, as explained previously was calculated using one or more incidences of (i) probation/parole technical violations, (ii) a warrant for absconding from probation/ parole, (iii) re-arrest of a new crime, (iv) re-conviction of a new crime, and (v) re-incarceration during a twelve month time period. This data should be considered comprehensive due to the use of multiple sources of data.

Probation/Parole Technical Violations

Based on a triangulation of data sources, almost 79% of all offenders in this study received a technical violation from their probation and/or parole officer during their progress in treatment. These statistics are comparable to other probation/ parole studies that indicate that as many as 70%-80% of offenders do not comply with the terms of their probation/ parole (Taxman and Cherkos, 1995; Cunniff, 1991).

Warrant for Arrest

Although most recidivism studies do not utilize an introspective variable within technical violations of probation/parole, the author chose to measure a more serious technical violation of an offender which resulted in a warrant for that offender's arrest. During the process of either ongoing *ATR* treatment and the first 12 months of release, approximately 17% of all offenders had a warrant charged for their arrest. As a result of this warrant, some of these offenders may have surrendered to their probation/ parole officer or police. Others would have been arrested, and could have been revoked to jail and/ or prison thereby dismissing them from the Lake City program. It is important to recognize that if an offender was dismissed from the program, the author still tracked the offender of potential technical violations and/or warrants.

Arrest for New Crime

An offender's arrest of a new crime was carefully constructed using a variety of sources of information. Utilizing offender self reporting, documentation from probation/ parole agencies and paperwork from correctional facilities in case files, re-arrest was calculated. Approximately 30% of all offenders were re-arrested while completing the *ATR* program and/or over the next 12 months after being released. Despite an offender's arrest, many of these offenders were not charged with new crimes and/or technical violations of their probation/parole. This percentage shadows the national averages which suggest that within the first six months of the 1994 national recidivism study that 30% were re-arrested for a felony or a serious misdemeanor (Langan and Levin, 2002:5). Although some might suggest that the participants in this study have lower recidivism rates simply because it is over the first year of being released from prison (rather than the first six months).

Conviction

With an expected lag time, it was necessary for the researcher to utilize State court database documentation to validate case file reviews. Approximately 16% of all offenders were re-convicted of a crime twelve months after being released. Compared to national 1994 BJS figures, this is similar but lower than the approximate 22% of offenders that were reconvicted nationally (Langan and Levin, 2002:5).

Incarceration

Of all offenders participating in the Lake City program, 23% were re-incarcerated in jail or prison either as a result of failing in their participation or as a result of being arrested or convicted of a crime. These percentages shadow the 1994 national study on recidivism identifying that approximately one-quarter of offenders released in 1994 had returned to either a state or federal prison as a result of another prison sentence (due to violating their probation/ parole or a new criminal activity). This also did not reflect offenders that were sentenced to jail time. This study substantiates that 22% of offenders were re-incarcerated (to jail and/or prison) for either a technical violation, or a conviction of new crime.

RESEARCH MODEL II

As explained in the literature review, the first research question of this study measured the efficacy of the Lake City ATR program in reducing offender recidivism. As explained in Chapters II and III, the researcher utilized potentially effective predictors of an offender's recidivism rates based on scholarly literature review.

The researcher conceptualized recidivism using five measurements: (i) one or more documented incidences of probation or parole violations; (ii) a warrant for non-compliance of an offender's terms of probation/ parole (which could include absconding from custody); (iii) re-arrest of a new crime; (iv) re-conviction of a new crime; and (v) re-incarceration of an offender. The tables within this section identify the predictive power of the logistic regression modeling on each of the five recidivism variables. In addition to the findings of the multivariate regression, the author also wanted to explore what, if any factors could be associated or related to an offender's success or failure of recidivism. This exploratory modeling would be possible because each of the five recidivism measurements were taken during two month intervals while offenders were completing the Lake City ATR treatment program.

Probation/Parole Technical Violations

Before completing each of the five logistical regression analyses, it was imperative to ensure that no multi-collinearity existed between the independent variables evaluated. Having evaluated the role, if any, multi-collinearity, the researcher proceeded to investigate the role of outliers on the analysis. Outliers with over a 2.0 residual, with further residuals above seven were removed from the analysis. For the purposes of these five research sub-questions, as many as two cases were removed for each of the regression analyses. This general approach to examining assumptions was used for each of the regression analyses.

Utilizing a logistic regression analysis, Table 9 illustrates the predictive power of twenty five variables on an offender's probation/parole technical violations.

Table 9 – Technical Violations

Variable of Interest	B	S.E.	Sig.	
Sex (male)	-0.82	0.31	.009	*
Age	0.01	0.02	.475	
Race (Black)	0.04	0.75	.958	
Ethnicity (Hispanic)	0.48	0.58	.410	
Marital status (Single)	-0.45	0.37	.222	
ASI	0.40	0.32	.214	
ASAM	-0.22	0.04	.624	
Level of care	0.29	0.20	.150	
Prevalent drug	0.69	1.17	.557	
Polymer drug	-0.08	0.41	.840	
Duration	0.84	0.10	.000	*
Abstinence	0.18	0.31	.561	
Faith based treatment	0.58	0.38	.133	
Religion (Catholic)	0.17	0.40	.096	
Case management	0.05	0.05	.285	
Informal support	0.58	0.62	.351	
Housing	-0.14	0.31	.640	
Health care	-0.14	0.32	.651	
Mental health	0.31	0.51	.561	
Employment	0.50	0.24	.040	*
Transportation	0.28	0.34	.420	
Clothing	-0.45	0.31	.887	
Education	-0.13	0.29	.660	
Years incarcerated	-0.01	0.05	.954	
Prior convictions	0.08	0.04	.063	
Constant	**-3.49**	**1.50**	**.020**	

Model -2 Log likelihood 293.940 Cox & Snell R Square .256
Nagelkerke R Square .341 Chi-square 79.826
Degrees of freedom 25 Model significance .000

The 25 variables within the model were found to explain approximately 34% (based on the Nagelkerke R-square) of the variance of technical violations. This allowed the author to reject the null hypothesis and conclude that not all of the model coefficients were equal to zero. This was verified using the Hosmer and Lemeshow test; which determined that there was a significant difference between predicted and observed values; also suggesting a reasonably good fit for the model and data. Furthermore, the model was found to be better at predicting a probation/parole violation (88%; 61%) during an offender's treatment in the Lake City *ATR* program.

Within the first regression model to study recidivism, only three variables: sex, the duration of time offender's spent in treatment and employment were found to be influential (with a confidence level of 95% with the $p < .05$ being significantly different than zero). Men were more likely than women to be technical violators of the terms of their probation and/or parole. The research model also found that the more time an offender spends in treatment, the less likely they will be violators of the terms of their probation/ parole. Offenders who were employed were less likely to be violators of the terms of their release.

Warrant for Arrest

Illustrated in Table 10 below is the predictive power of 25 variables to explain an offender being issued a warrant for offender arrest. Overall, these variables within the model were found to explain approximately 20% (based on the Nagelkerke R-square) of the variance of an offender receiving a warrant for their arrest. This allowed the author to reject the null hypothesis and conclude that all of the model coefficients are not equal to zero. As seen below, six variables were found to have predictive power of a warrant issued for an offender's arrest.

As explained previously, six variables; sex, the ASI clinical instrument (documenting risk of the offender), the type of drug most prevalently used by an offender, the duration of treatment, whether an offender received employment, and the amount of funding an offender received for housing were found to be significant. Men participating in the Lake City program were more likely than women to be issued a warrant for their arrest. The ASI clinical instrument (as explained in more depth in chapters 2 and 3) was a good predictor of offenders receiving a warrant for their arrest.

Consequently, an offender who scored high on a risk assessment was more likely to receive a warrant for his/ her arrest. Another variable of interest was whether an offender's type of drug prevalence may have an effect on recidivism. It was found that any drug other than alcohol and marijuana were more likely to warrant an arrest to detain. The duration in months that an offender spent within their treatment programming was also found to be a statistically significant predictor in whether an offender would receive a warrant. Those offenders who remained in treatment for longer lengths of time were less likely to receive a warrant for their arrest. Employment, as expected, was also found to be the best predictor (via the Beta value) of whether an offender would receive a warrant for their arrest. Therefore, if an offender was employed, they were less likely to receive a warrant for their arrest. In addition, it would only make sense that if the *ATR* program were paying for an offender, those offenders would be less likely to receive a warrant for their arrest (usually because they would not be absconding from their probation/parole officers).

For those offenders completing twelve months of *ATR* programming, approximately 10% of these offenders received a warrant for their arrest within the first two months. However, as offenders continued through the programming, there was a significant reduction of warrants issued. Within the third and fourth months, 5% (n=26) of offenders received a warrant for their arrest. After the first four months, there was a significant drop off in warrants issued from 26 offenders (5%) in the third and fourth month to 5 offenders (2%) in months five and six; to only 2 more warrants issued between the seventh and twelfth months. This finding would suggest that the longer offenders complete treatment, the less likely they will receive a warrant issued for their arrest.

Table 10 – Warrant Issued for Arrest

Variable of Interest	B	S.E.	Sig.	
Sex (male)	0.74	0.35	.035	*
Age	0.01	0.02	.740	
Race (Black)	- 0.01	0.27	.972	
Ethnicity(Hispanic)	- 0.20	0.57	.730	
Marital status (single)	0.13	0.38	.733	
ASI	0.26	0.19	.168	*
ASAM	- 0.20	0.04	.562	
Level of care	- 0.10	0.20	.622	
Prevalent drug (marijuana)	- 0.39	0.31	.214	*
Polymer drug	0.04	0.17	.829	
Duration	1.02	0.06	.032	*
Abstinence	- 0.31	0.28	.273	
Faith based treatment	- 0.01	0.34	.980	
Religion (Catholic)	- 0.14	0.08	.072	
Case management	0.00	0.05	.995	
Informal support	0.25	0.38	.518	
Housing	0.35	0.30	.046	*
Health care	0.27	0.63	.595	
Mental health	0.26	0.45	.467	
Employment	2.21	0.27	.003	*
Transportation	- 0.14	0.31	.913	
Clothing	0.15	0.05	.777	
Education	- 0.06	0.09	.511	
Years incarcerated	- 0.01	0.49	.993	
Prior convictions	0.01	0.04	.831	
Constant	**-3.646**	**1.69**	**.031**	*

Model -2 Log likelihood 212.091 Cox & Snell R Square .120
Nagelkerke R Square .200 Chi-square 34.404
Degrees of freedom 25 Model significance .007

Arrest

Table 11 clearly identifies that the twenty-five variables explained 64% (based on the Nagelkerke R-square) of the variance of an offender's re-arrest while completing the Lake City program.

Table 11 – Arrest

Variable of Interest	B	S.E.	Sig.	
Sex (male)	-0.26	0.35	.465	
Age	-0.01	0.02	.824	
Race (Black)	-0.10	0.32	.761	
Ethnicity(Hispanic)	0.36	0.64	.579	
Marital status (single)	0.56	0.47	.229	
ASI	1.20	0.35	.005	*
ASAM	0.21	0.06	.945	
Level of care	0.09	0.22	.664	
Prevalent drug (marijuana)	-0.32	0.20	.050	*
Polymer drug	0.54	0.61	.011	*
Duration	0.06	0.07	.000	*
Abstinence	0.51	0.38	.640	
Faith based treatment	-0.88	0.44	.491	
Religion (Catholic)	-0.06	0.09	.471	
Case management	0.07	0.06	.221	
Informal support	0.63	0.07	.645	
Housing	0.84	0.14	.087	
Health care	0.51	0.28	.000	*
Mental health	0.76	0.89	.619	
Employment	0.41	0.28	.140	
Transportation	0.19	0.58	.292	
Clothing	0.04	0.06	.583	
Education	-0.07	0.10	.458	
Years incarcerated	0.28	0.56	.615	
Prior convictions	-0.01	0.05	.782	
Constant	**-7.10**	**1.89**	**.000**	*

Model -2 Log likelihood 265.526 Cox & Snell R Square .454
Nagelkerke R Square .644 Chi-square 53.528
Degrees of freedom 25 Model significance .000

Five variables were found to be significant: predictors of offender arrest: an offender's aggregate ASI risk assessment, the type of drug use, offender polymer drug use, the duration within *ATR* treatment, and whether an offender received medical assistance. Similar to the previous logistic model, it seems that the ASI is a good predictor of arrest as a measure of recidivism. Based on offender's self reporting of drug abuse, it seems that the more dangerous type of drug abuse (crack/cocaine/heroine) and their polymer usage has an effect on whether they will be arrested for such usage. The longer the length of time an offender spends within their *ATR* treatment means the lower likelihood they would be re- arrested. Interestingly, when an offender received medical assistance as a resource of the ATR program, they would be less likely to be re-arrested

For those offenders completing twelve months of *ATR* programming, approximately 15% of these offenders were arrested within the first two months. As offenders progressed through the program, there was a significant decline in offender re-arrests. Within the third and fourth months, 11% of offenders were re-arrested. After the first four months, there were more significant reductions. Less than 5% of offenders were re-arrested in months five and six, and only three of 270 offenders were arrested between months seven and twelve. This was an interesting finding. This finding would make the argument that sustained treatment significantly reduces an offender's likelihood of arrest.

Conviction

Conviction was the fourth of five recidivism research models used to explain the predictive power of re-conviction of a new crime. This model has a relatively lower level of explanative power than arrest (37%; based on the Nagelkerke R-square). Six variables: an offender's race and ethnicity, their ASI risk assessment score, prevalent and polymer drug use, and duration of time in treatment were found to be significant predictors of offender conviction. Blacks were more likely than any other categorical group (Whites, Asians, Native Americans) to be convicted of a new crime. Another demographic variable, an offender being of Hispanic culture was more likely to be convicted of a crime than someone who did not identify to being Hispanic. Without being repetitive, it seems that the ASI clinical tool for practitioners was a terrific predictor of recidivism (from warrants for arrest, to arrest and now, conviction of a new crime). The type of drug usage by offenders also seemed to have negative consequences. Offenders who were more likely to use dangerous drugs such as crack/cocaine and heroin were more likely than alcohol and marijuana users to be convicted of a new crime. Also pertinent, was whether an offender used multiple drugs within the same occasion. It seems that the effect of doing more dangerous drugs in combination had an effect on the conviction measurement of recidivism. The findings from the logistic regression also identify an offender's treatment duration as a significant predictor of conviction. Therefore, the longer the offender remains in treatment, the less likely they may be arrested and/or convicted of a new crime. These statistics can be located in Table 12 below.

Of those offenders completing twelve months of *ATR* programming, very few offenders were sent churning through the criminal justice system. Only 36 of 270 offenders were convicted of a previous or new crime. Within the first four months of participating in the program, 5% of offenders were convicted of a previous or new crime.

As explained previously, it was highly unlikely that offenders would be admitted to *ATR* program immediately upon release from prison. Therefore, it was possible that charges could have been laid either when an offender was still in prison, newly released, or while participating through the Lake City program. Offenders convicted were significantly reduced over the following months. This would suggest that after the first four months of treatment, offenders are less likely to be involved in criminal behavior, and also less likely to be convicted of a previous or new charge.

Table 12 – Conviction

Variable of Interest	B	S.E.	Sig.	
Sex (male)	-0.08	0.32	.800	
Age	-0.01	0.02	.445	
Race (Black)	0.62	0.30	.037	*
Ethnicity(Hispanic)	0.15	0.58	.791	*
Marital status (single)	-0.08	0.41	.847	
ASI	0.25	0.08	.020	*
ASAM	0.48	0.11	.825	
Level of care	-0.16	0.20	.434	
Prevalent drug (marijuana)	0.36	0.17	.037	*
Polymer drug	0.82	0.56	.041	*
Duration	-0.13	0.07	.046	*
Abstinence	0.84	0.38	.416	
Faith based treatment	-0.30	0.37	.436	
Religion (Catholic)	-0.03	0.08	.747	
Case management	0.00	0.05	.990	
Informal support	-0.52	0.03	.826	
Housing	0.20	0.01	.129	
Health care	0.54	0.35	.852	
Mental health	-1.24	0.61	.663	
Employment	-0.04	0.26	.866	
Transportation	0.29	0.06	.725	
Clothing	0.83	0.01	.186	
Education	-0.15	0.09	.107	
Years incarcerated	-0.39	0.47	.408	
Prior convictions	-0.06	0.05	.204	
Constant	-3.00	1.81	.097	

Model -2 Log likelihood 148.083 Cox & Snell R Square .200
Nagelkerke R Square .372 Chi-square 60.206
Degrees of freedom 25 Model significance .001

Incarceration

Incarceration was the fifth research model of recidivism that the author was interested in. Table 13 illustrates the predictive power of twenty-five variables to explain offender incarceration using logistic regression. Although significant, the model was not a very good predictor of the outcome of offender incarceration (29% based on Nagelkerke R-Square).

Five variables were found to be statistically significant predictor of incarceration. These variables include: an offender's ethnicity (identified as being Hispanic), the duration of their treatment within the ATR program, an offender's case manager, whether an offender received employment and the funds used to assist offenders with transportation. Those offenders identifying as being Hispanic were more likely to be incarcerated during their progress throughout the ATR program. Similar to each logistic regression model, the duration of an offender's treatment program was a predictor in their incarceration to jail and/or prison. The longer an offender remained in the treatment program, the less likely the offender would return to jail and/or prison. As explained in the literature review, case managers often have a great deal of discretion when working with probation/parole officers and other networked criminal justice practitioners. Therefore, case managers could be important predictors of determining an offender's track towards reintegration into the community. If an offender was employed, they would be less likely to be re-incarcerated.

Of the 270 offenders completing twelve months of *ATR* programming, approximately 9% of these offenders were re-incarcerated within the first two months. Incarceration could include being detained in jail or being sent back to prison for a longer and extended period of time, in which the offender would be released from the Lake City program.

During the second interval, three to four months, an additional 9% of offenders were incarcerated. During months five and six, 7% of offenders returned to jail or prison. After month six, only one offender was incarcerated. The data suggests that long sustained treatment (longer than six months) results in a lesser likelihood of offender incarceration.

Table 13– Incarceration

Variable of Interest	B	S.E.	Sig.	
Sex (male)	- 0.09	0.30	.703	
Age	- 0.02	0.02	.330	
Race (Black)	0.02	0.25	.583	
Ethnicity(Hispanic)	- 1.05	0.63	.045	*
Marital status (single)	0.14	0.36	.137	
ASI	0.23	0.03	.364	
ASAM	0.84	0.51	.482	
Level of care	0.34	0.18	.706	
Prevalent drug (marijuana)	- 0.07	0.16	.183	
Polymer drug	- 0.16	0.42	.975	
Duration	0.05	0.06	.001	*
Abstinence	0.35	0.28	.971	
Faith based treatment	0.44	0.33	.228	
Religion (Catholic)	0.05	0.07	.982	
Case management	- 0.11	0.05	.044	*
Informal support	0.82	0.34	.555	
Housing	0.35	0.06	.716	
Health care	0.29	0.23	.225	
Mental health	0.43	0.09	.940	
Employment	- 0.18	0.24	.047	*
Transportation	0.61	0.42	.047	*
Clothing	0.58	0.07	.395	
Education	0.08	0.09	.367	
Years incarcerated	- 0.19	0.44	.844	
Prior convictions	- 0.02	0.04	.812	
Constant	**- 2.99**	**1.35**	**.028**	

Model -2 Log likelihood 229.832 Cox & Snell R Square .188
Nagelkerke R Square .289 Chi-square 9.539
Degrees of freedom 25 Model significance .000

OVERALL MODEL FINDINGS

The findings of the research modeling identify a select number of predictors that were able to have explanatory power in explaining offender recidivism and offender success within the Lake City program. As explained in the research models, the effect of the *ATR* program seemed to have had very little to no significant impact on an offender's recidivism. Deductively (based on the Cox regression), there were interesting findings to suggest that time in treatment had some effects on recidivism but these factors were not statistically significant.

Subsequently (based on these analyses) there are inconsistencies that would suggest that more in-depth research needs to be conducted over the remaining two years of data collection for the Lake City program to determine its successes and/or failures. Based on the preliminary data (this first year of the *ATR* program's operation), there should be cautious optimism that progress is being made. If approximately one out of every five offenders were completing the program successfully, it may be implied that the inclusion of case managers, an informal support system and AODA treatment may reduce criminal activity.

In addition to completing multivariate analysis, the author was also interested in offender characteristics and/or factors that might influence an offender's success and/or failure in the *ATR* program. To answer this question, it was necessary to recode the dependent and independent variables to complete a Cox regression model.

The purpose of using the Cox (1972) regression model for this study examined the cumulative survival function of offenders within the Lake City program. For the purposes of exploration, it was necessary to use the Cox proportion hazards model because multiple linear regressions do not allow for analysis on time to event data of the kind that the researcher was analyzing. The problem involved those cases that are censored. "Censored" in this context means that an offender who succeeds after that sixth point (twelve months or the final point in the study) was not fully accounted for with ordinary regression approaches: this person would be a censored case.

When checking the proportional hazards assumption, it was necessary to determine whether the hazard for one case was the same over time when compared to other cases. Therefore, the data should have indicated randomness. However, this was not the case. For a majority of variables within the Cox modeling for all seven models, there was no randomness, indicating that the data was violating the assumptions of the Cox survival analysis.

Based on the findings of the Cox proportional modeling, there were no significant factors that influenced an offender's success or failure within the Lake City program. This was a significant finding in and of itself. The purpose of the Lake City *ATR* program was to develop a holistic and individualized program for each offender. Based on this assumption it was possible that the author was not able to collect other relevant factors of interest that could be psychological in nature (i.e. an offender's motivation to complete treatment and/or stress factors). Therefore, all further discussion will simply examine the frequency distributions of offender's potential criminal behavior throughout their participation in the AODA program in Lake City.

CHAPTER 5:

Conclusions and Recommendations

There were several conclusions that promote the use of a systems based approach, which was utilized in Lake City's *Access To Recovery* (*ATR*) alcohol and other drug abuse (AODA) program. This systems based approach which focused on individualistic and holistic approaches to treatment also had a significant effect on recidivism. This section highlights ten significant conclusions evaluating the Lake City *ATR* program and potential recommendations for the future study of offender reintegration.

CONCLUSIONS

1. The self reported high risk drug offender in the *ATR* program had a significantly higher likelihood of program failure and criminal activity.

For the purpose of this discussion, the author would articulate a high risk drug offender to be using cocaine/crack or heroin in combination with one another and alcohol use. These particular offenders were found to have significantly higher likelihoods of program failure, a warrant served for their arrest, to be arrested, and to be convicted of a new crime. The author would likely suggest, as others have, that more attention should be placed on these offenders and that rather than offenders are given options of outpatient or intensive inpatient care for their AODA, they are simply expected to go into residential treatment centers, which would allow them more opportunity to slowly reintegrate into the community and perhaps reduce their dangerous drug abuse behavior and likelihood of criminal activity.

2. An offender's increased duration in AODA programming resulted in higher likelihoods of remaining abstinent and reducing recidivism.

An offender's duration was the single most important factor found to be statistically significant throughout all the logistic regression models. Therefore, the more committed an offender was to completing long term treatment provisions, the more likely the offender would be successful in remaining abstinent and being successful in completion on the Lake City program. This also yielded significant benefits for an offender's likelihood of recidivism. Statistics in this study indicate that those offenders who chose to remain compliant with their AODA programming for longer periods of time would likely refrain and/or desist from criminal activity (from technical violations to incarceration) within their first year of returning to their communities. The percentage of offenders who completed the program successfully and consequently reduced their likelihood of recidivism were at the lower end of the spectrum (less than 20%) over the first year of tracking. One might look at these numbers and suggest that 20% is poor and that the program should be cancelled. Others could examine the percentages and find cause for success and vindication. Others could simply make political statements about the appropriate or misappropriate purposes of spending large sums of money to assist offenders reintegrate into their communities. While these numbers do not articulate significant reductions in AODA and recidivism, there should be cause for hope. It is this author's opinion that the process of implementation (which was not measured within this study) might identify significant changes that can be made to better outcomes for offenders returning to the community.

3. Faith based programming was not found to be an effective predictor in increasing treatment outcomes nor, reducing an offender's likelihood of recidivism.

When President George W. Bush announced in his 2004 State of the Union Address for *ATR*, the initiative would provide offenders seeking drug and alcohol treatment with vouchers to pay for a range of appropriate community and faith based services (SAMHSA, 2006). Based on this evaluation, 19% of all offenders within the Lake City program who received faith based services from community and treatment providers were no more or less likely to have a reduced likelihood of recidivism nor, were these offenders more successful in completing the program.

Although the literature review of faith based treatment and programming is still emerging, the majority of literature indicates that religion influences various forms of delinquency, deviance and crime. Religion has been empirically linked to restrain delinquent behavior; thus, it is logical to conclude that religion can assist in offender rehabilitation (Workman, 2005). Therefore, in theory, any spiritual transformation may act as a turning point in an offender's life which can lead to a desistance from crime.

Within the limitations of this study, faith based programming did not have an effect on reducing AODA or criminal activity. This could be due to the variance of treatment programming itself, in that each treatment provider and/or facilitator may have different approaches to reducing AODA. The author would insist that more direct observation of these programming modalities could assist in determining the potential effectiveness of each treatment provider (which was beyond the scope of this study).

4. An offender's informal support system was a good predictor in increasing an offender's success within treatment.

An offender's informal support system, such as family, friends and non-governmental organizations are the systems that will be in place long after an offender's completion of treatment and/or probation/ parole supervision. The presence and influence of an offender's informal support system was found to be a significant predictor of both an offender's abstinence while completing treatment and an offender's successful completion in the Lake City program. This positive correlation would suggest that family and friends are keys in understanding correctional reintegration. The Lake City program, like other systems approaches to alcohol and other drug abuse (AODA) treatment programs is based on a holistic approach. This approach was designed to utilize an offender's informal social support system, rather than simply being forced by formal support mechanisms, such as police, courts and correctional personnel. The author would suggest that more correctional systems consider or adopt a holistic RST (recovery support team) approach to reintegration so that probation/parole officers are able to learn more about how offenders respond in their own environment with their family and friends. This can lead to better outcome measures for AODA and potential desistence from criminal activity.

5. **Case managers played a significant role as a predictor of both an offender's success in AODA treatment and likelihood of being re-incarcerated.**

As explained in the three logistic regression models in the previous chapter, case management was found to be a significant predictor of an offender's abstinence from alcohol and other drug abuse, an offender's success within the *ATR* program, and an offender's re-incarceration to jail and/or prison. This was consistent with other treatment programs and the findings of previous research. The author would argue that further research should focus on the direct effects, influence and discretion case managers have in assisting their offenders and the relationships they develop with formal social control agents (law enforcement, court officials and attorneys, probation/ parole officers, correctional social workers). Increased dialogue and communication within these unique bureaucracies could close gaps in information sharing and better the outcomes of offenders.

6. **An integrated systems approach was effective to provide the adequate resources for offenders reintegrating into their communities.**

As explained in the literature review, offender reintegration within a systems approach would target each individual offender's areas of need or risk while completing some form of AODA/behavioral/cognitive treatment. In addition to completing

AODA treatment, this study found that offenders had significant needs that were met by the *ATR* program. As states across the country trim their budgets, they may also be reducing the resources of community based corrections, and the ancillary services offenders need. Many offenders leave prison without any housing, employment, or long term planning. Compounding this problem were the large numbers of offenders churning through the system and the lack of funding available for community based corrections (versus institutional corrections).

The results of this study found that an overwhelming percentage of offenders (93%) participating in the Lake City program received grant assistance for housing, employment, and other ancillary services. Half or 50% of offenders who participated in the *ATR* program received some form of housing assistance based on a voucher program. Of the 434 offenders enrolled in the program studied, approximately 152, or 35% received funding which resulted in six to twelve months of free medical/ emergency care within the state system. Approximately 9% of all offenders within Lake City's program reported a mental illness and all received a diagnosis through the County's mental health clinic. Almost half of all offenders (43%) received some form of employment assistance of which nearly half (41%) attained part time or full time employment if even for a brief point in time during their participation in the ATR program. Of the 434 offenders enrolled in the *ATR* program, a majority of offenders simply did not have the resources to acquire adequate transportation to and from their treatment appointments, probation/ parole officer meetings, a job, or vocational training. As a result, 68% of all offenders received some transportation assistance which likely had a direct effect on other success outcome measurements. Once released from jail and/or prison, many of the *ATR* offenders have little to no resources. In many cases, offenders left their prison cell with only the clothes they had when they were first admitted to prison. Therefore, many offenders had immediate personal hygiene and clothing needs. Of 434 offenders, 249 offenders, or 58% received some form of clothing and/or personal care needs allowances. Based solely on these statistics, there is no discounting that any resources that offenders received likely had a direct or indirect effect on the treatment and recidivism outcomes.

While many of these funding allocations were not statistically significant, the author would argue that a majority of monies to assist offender programming (say 75%) should be utilized towards actually funding offender assistance rather than funding bureaucracies, special interest groups, evaluation consultants, project managers, travel costs to conferences, etc. This may result in more statistically significant outcomes.

7. There were few statistically significant predictors of Lake City's *ATR* program.

Based on the results of the multivariate analyses, few variables were found to be significant predictors of offender recidivism or offender success/ failure within the Lake City program. This was not necessarily a surprise.

The author expected that several variables within each model would be significant. However, the author would argue that one possible reason the models did not account for larger variances being explained was due to the holistic and individualist nature of the program. Due to this approach, each offender (while having the opportunity to receive similar grant assistance) has unique risks factors which should result in different treatment or single coordinated care plans (SCCP). While this author would argue that the outcome measures used in this study were reliable and valid, more attention should be paid to the conceptualization and operationalization of realistic and observable measurements of success within the Lake City *ATR* programming before the program is implemented. This would allow for more accurate evaluations to be completed through the duration of this three year grant. In addition, the researcher would suggest that these databases be shared and merged with Department of Corrections databases to find adequate experimental and control groups, to better determine how a limited amount of resources should be shared and/or utilized.

8. The Addiction Severity Index (ASI) was identified as being a very good predictor of this study's measurements of recidivism.

While the ASI is widely used for alcohol and drug assessment, it was a better and statistically significant predictor of criminal activity that would result in a warrant for an arrest of an offender, arrest of an offender, and the conviction of an offender. The author was simply shocked that this tool was so effective in predicting recidivism. As explained previously, studies have shown a relationship between AODA and crime but perhaps it is this risk assessment tool that could be utilized to examine the potential of criminal activity. Based on the ASI assessment tool, offenders were found to have needed assistance for: medical (45%), employment (98%), alcohol (66%), drugs (78%), legal (66%), family (59%), and psychological/ mental health assistance (59%). This is significantly different than what each offender received while in the ATR program so it could be argued that the ATR program simply didn't provide many of the needed services to each offender or the offender chose not to utilize those services. Perhaps, if these services were allocated and utilized by offenders, the ASI would have been a better predictive tool than a screening tool for clinicians. The author would suggest that more research should be done on the predictive power on the ASI instrument.

9. Churning remains a problem for Lake City correctional administrators.

As explained in the literature review and this study's findings chapter, offender prior records and convictions suggest that churning continues to take place within the State's correctional facilities. Data from the State's court database found that the median number of convictions for offenders participating in the Lake City program was five. However, 23% of offenders had between six and ten convictions, and 9.2% had 11 or more convictions. Further analysis of the data found that approximately 6% of all offenders had spent less than six months in jail and/or prison. The median time that offenders were incarcerated, prior to their enrollment in the *ATR* program was approximately four years. This leads the author to believe that within their lifetime, offenders are continuing their cycling trends through the State's correctional facilities.

10. The recidivism in Lake City shadowed national recidivism rates.

Denoted above, churning continues to be a significant problem for State correctional administrators. This churning was a direct result of incidences of recidivism over a possible twelve months of *ATR* treatment and case management services: (i) probation/ parole technical violations, (ii) warrants for absconding from probation/parole, (iii) arrest, (iv) conviction, and (v) incarceration. The findings support the fact that Lake City had similar recidivism rates as the 1994 national recidivism study by the Bureau of Justice Statistics (Langan and Levin, 2002).

Exactly 70% of all offenders received a technical violation from their probation and/ or parole officer during their time in the Lake City *ATR* treatment program. This was consistent with previous studies completed by Landis *et al.* (1969), Langan and Levin (2002) and Taxman and Cherkos (1995).

Based on absconding from probation/ parole (certainly a technical violation), approximately 17% of all *ATR* offenders were served with a warrant for their arrest. Some of these offenders may have surrendered to their probation/ parole officer or police while others would have been apprehended and arrested. While this measurement has never been used as a measurement of recidivism (after a comprehensive literature review), the author was interested in any new measurements that could be utilized to understand the complexity of recidivism. While completing this particular study, the author found it extremely difficult to ascertain whether probation/parole agents were aware of an offender's contact with law enforcement. It was for this reason that the author chose to examine a warrant for arrest variable which could explain the difference and/or intermediate step between the arrest of an offender due to a probation/parole offense and the arrest of an offender for a new crime (which are two unique variables). Similar to the new Bureau of Justice statistics recidivism research, the author would insist that we need to examine the reasons for a new arrest (as it is considered the most effective measurement of recidivism).

While many offenders reported police contact, approximately 30% of all offenders were re-arrested while completing the Lake City program. This percentage was similar to that of the 1994 national recidivism study completed by the Bureau of Justice Statistics. Langan and Levin reported that within the first six months of an offender's release, approximately 30% of the 272,111 offenders were re-arrested for a felony or a serious misdemeanor (2002:1). After one year, the cumulative total grew to 44%, by the second year 60%, and three year tracking found 67.5% of the 272,111 released prisoners were re-arrested (at least once).

Based on the findings of the data, with respect to some expected lag time, approximately 16% of all offenders were re-convicted of a new crime. Unfortunately, it was difficult to determine if this crime was a new crime, or a crime committed during the one to two week interval before the offender entered into the Lake City treatment program. This was similar to the 1994 Bureau of Justice Statistics national report on recidivism. Langan and Levin (2002) reported that within the first year of an offender's release, approximately 22% of the 272,111 released offenders were re-convicted for a new misdemeanor or felony.

The data supported that a minority of offenders in this study were involved in the re-arrest, re-conviction and re-incarceration process. However, 23% or 103 of 434 offenders were re-incarcerated during their involvement within the *ATR* program. This may include re-incarceration in jail or prison for technical violations to their probation/parole or based on new arrests or convictions. These percentages shadow the 26% of first year released offenders in 1994 that had returned to either a state or federal prison (Langan and Levin, 2002).

Taking into account, that the median time in which offenders participated in the Lake City program was only five months, the percentages of recidivism could only be expected to increase with time. Most studies (including the national studies examined in the literature review) examine recidivism at one, two or three year intervals. This study can say with certainty, that these recidivism rates are occurring within the first five to six months after being released. Therefore, one could argue that recidivism rates in Lake City are similar or higher than national recidivism rates.

RECOMMENDATIONS FOR FUTURE RESEARCH

In 1971, David Rothman, one of the foremost authorities on the history and development of the prison system, wrote that "we have been gradually emerging from institutional responses and one can foresee the period when incarceration will be used still more rarely than it is today" (Rothman, 1971:2). Perhaps Rothman simply envisioned an America as many of us do, where incarceration to jail and/or prison should only be utilized for its initial purpose – to isolate dangerous offenders from the communities in which they could not remain orderly in. Perhaps that is the goal of many practitioners and academics. However, the reality is that the United States incarcerates more people within any given day than any other country in the world. As Austin explains, we are in an "incarceration binge" led industry (2001:1).

Only two years after Rothman wrote his vision of incarceration, the National Advisory Commission on Criminal Justice Standards and Goals, concluded that "the prison, the reformatory and the jail have achieved only a shocking record of failure," (Mauer, 2001; National Advisory Commission, 1973: 597) recommending that "no new institutions for adults should be built and existing institutions for juveniles should be closed" (National Advisory Commission, 1973: 358).

We know what works. Without being repetitive, theoretically sound and empirically based principles have been identified. Studies completed by Andrews (1995; 1990), Cullen and Gendreau (2000), Mackenzie (1997) and Sherman *et al.* (1997) all identify that (i) treatment should identify risk factors; (ii) programs should employ cognitive-behavioral, skills-oriented, or multimodal treatment approaches; (iii) interventions should focus on the needs of the participant; and (iv) treatment interventions should be implemented appropriately in a well supportive environment. This *ATR* program was one of many faith based initiatives designed to utilize all four of these empirically based principles. Still the outcomes fall short of our expectations. So then, where can be targeted for future research?

Based on the findings of the data, when several millions of dollars are allocated for pilot programs such as the Lake City *ATR* program, more detail needs to be placed on research designs and the triangulation of methodologies. As Sherman *et al.* (1997) explain, few studies are able to utilize true experimental designs. Practitioners and academics should work together to ensure that research designs include both valid and reliable process and outcome measurements (before the program begins). Collaborating together would allow for more streams of research to be collected on both a qualitative and quantitative level. This one suggestion alone, in the author's opinion, would result in renewed progress between practitioners and academics in the understanding the complexities of alcohol and other drug abuse treatment, and its relationship with crime. This would further assist our understanding of the complexities that offenders face when reintegrating back into their communities and develop effective programming to assist them.

Bibliography

Adams, K., K. Bennett, J. Flanagan, J. Marquart, S. Cuvelier, E. Fritsch, J. Gerber, D. Longmire and V. Burton. 1994. "A Large-Scale Multidimensional Test of the Effect of Prison Education Programs on Offenders Behavior." *The Prison Journal* 74(4): 433–50.

Allen, Francis. 1981. *The Decline of the Rehabilitative Ideal: Penal Policy and Social Purpose*. New Haven, CT: Yale University Press.

American Correctional Association. *The Corrections Compendium Survey – 2003*. Date Retrieved: March 19, 2006: http://www.aca.org/publications/cctopics.asp

American Society of Addiction Medicine (ASAM). Second Edition -Revised of Patient Placement Criteria (ASAM PPC-2R). Retrieved: February 1, 2008: http://americ20.temp.veriohosting.com/ppc/ppc2.htm.

Andrews, D., I. Zinger, R. Hoge, J. Bonta, P. Gendreau and F. Cullen. 1990. "Does Correctional Treatment Work? A Clinically Relevant and Psychologically Informed Meta-analysis." *Criminology* 28, 369-404.

Andrews, Don and James Bonta. 1998. *The Psychology of Criminal Conduct, 2nd edition.* Cincinnati OH: Anderson Publishing.

Aos, S., M. Miller, and E. Drake. 2006. "*Evidence Based Adult Corrections Programs: What Works and What Does Not.*" Olympia, WA: Washington State Institute for Public Policy.

Arfken, C., C. Klein, E. Agius, and S. Menza. 2003. "Implementation of selected Target Cities components: Analysis of matching, case management, and linkages." In R. Stephens *et al.*, (eds.) *Clinical Assessment and Substance Abuse Treatment: The Target Cities Experience*. Albany: State University of New York Press.

Astbury, Brad. 2008. "Problems of Implementing Offender Programs in the Community". *Journal of Offender Rehabilitation*, 46: 31-47.

Austin, James. 2001. "Prisoner reentry: Current trends, practices, and issues." *Crime and Delinquency 47*: 314-334.

Austin, James and John Irwin. 2001. *It's About Time: America's Imprisonment Binge, 3rd edition*. Belmont, CA: Wadsworth.

Austin, C. and R. McLelland. 1994. "Case management in human services: Reflections on public policy." *Journal of Case Management 6*:119-126.

Barajas, Eduardo. 2000. *National Institute of Corrections Focus: High Risk Offenders in the Community*. U.S. Department of Justice. Washington, DC: National Institute of Corrections.

Barry, Kirsten. 1999. *Brief Interventions and Brief Therapies for Substance Abuse Treatment Improvement Protocol (TIP) Series 34*. Date Retrieved: January 16, 2006: http://ncadi.samhsa.gov/govpubs/BKD341/.

Bauer, Lynn. 2002. *Justice Expenditure and Employment in the United States*. U.S. Department of Justice. Washington, DC: Bureau of Justice Statistics.

Beck, Aaron. 2000. *State and Federal Prisoners Returning to the Community: Findings from the Bureau of Justice Statistics*. U.S. Department of Justice. Washington D.C.: Bureau of Justice Statistics.

Beck, Aaron. and Christopher Mumola. 1999. *Prisoners in 1998*. U.S. Department of Justice. Washington, D.C.: Bureau of Justice Statistics.

Beck, Aaron and Paige Harrison. 2001. *Prisoners in 2000*. U.S. Department of Justice. Washington, D.C.: Bureau of Justice Statistics.

Beck, Aaron and Laura Maruschak. 2001. *Mental Health Treatment in State Prisons*. U.S. Department of Justice. Washington, D.C.: Bureau of Justice Statistics.

Beck, Allen and Bernard Shipley. 1989. *Recidivism of Prisoners Released in 1983*. U.S. Department of Justice. Washington D.C.: Bureau of Justice Statistics.

Belenko, Steven. 1998. *Research on drug courts: A critical review*. New York: Columbia University. National Center on Addiction and Substance Abuse.

Belenko, Steven. 2000. "Diversion programs: Providing treatment-based alternatives to incarceration for drug-involved criminal offenders." *Connection 12:* 1-2, 8.

Belenko, S., M. Lang, and L. O'Connor. 2003. "Self-reported psychiatric treatment needs among felony drug offenders." *Journal of Contemporary Criminal Justice 19*(1), 9-29.

Belenko, S., C. Foltz, M. Lang, and H. E. Sung. 2004. "The impact on recidivism of residential treatment for high-risk drug felons: A longitudinal analysis." *Journal of Offender Rehabilitation 40*: 105-132.

Belenko, Steven and J. Peugh. 2005. "Estimating drug treatment needs among state prison inmates." *Drug and Alcohol Dependence 77*: 269-281.

Benedict, W. and L. Huff-Corzine. 1997. "Return to the scene of the punishment: recidivism of adult male property offenders on felony probation 1986-1989". *Journal of Research in Crime and Delinquency* 34:237-252.

Bernstein, Jared and Ellen Houston. 2001. *Crime and Work: What We Can Learn from the low-wage Labor Market*. Washington, DC: Economic Policy Institute.

Bloom, H., L. Orr, F. Doolitte, V. Hotz and B. Barnow. 1990. *Design of the National JTPA Study*. New York, NY: Manpower Demonstration Research Corporation.

Bloom, H., L..Orr, G. Cave, S. Bell, F. Doolittle, and W. Lin. 1994. *The National JTPA Study Overview: Impacts, Benefits, and Costs of Title II-A*. Bethesda, MD: Abt Associates, Inc.

Blumstein, Alfred, and Allen Beck. 1999. "Population Growth in U.S. Prisons, 1980-1996." *Crime and Justice: A Review of Research* 26:17.

Bonczar, Thomas and Lauren Glaze. 1999. *Probation and Parole in the United States, 1998*. U.S. Department of Justice. Washington, DC: Bureau of Justice Statistics.

Boyd-Franklin, N. 1989. *Black families in therapy: A multi-systems approach*. New York: Guilford Press.

Burnside, J., N. Loucks, J. R. Addler, and G. Rose. 2005. *My brother's keeper: Faith-based units in prison.* Cullompton, Devon, U.K.: Willan Publishing.

Burt, M., L. Aron, E. Lee, and J. Valente. 1999. *Helping America's homeless: Emergency shelter or affordable housing?* Washington, DC: Urban Institute.

Byrne, James. 1989. "Re-Integrating the Concept of Community into Community-Based Corrections." *Crime and Delinquency 35:* 471-499.

Byrne, J., A.J. Lurigio and J. Petersilia. 1992. *Smart Sentencing: The Emergence of Intermediate Sanctions*. Newbury Park, CA.: Sage Publishing Co.

Camp. S., J. Klein-Saffran, O. Kwon, D. Daggett and V. Joseph. 2006. "An Exploration into Participation in a Faith-Based Prison Program." *Criminology and Public Policy*. 5(3):529-550.

Camp, Camille and George Camp. 1997. *The corrections yearbook*. South Salem, NY: Criminal Justice Institute.

Camp, Camille and George Camp. 1999. *The Corrections Yearbook 1998.* Middletown, CT: Criminal Justice Institute.

Campbell, Donald and J. Stanley. 1963. *Experimental and quasi-experimental designs for research*. Chicago: Rand-McNally.

Center on Addiction and Substance Abuse. 1998. *Behind bars: Substance abuse and America's prison population.* New York: Center on Addiction and Substance Abuse.

Center for Disease Control. 2006. *Alcohol-attributable deaths and years of potential life lost - United States, 2005. Morbidity and Mortality Weekly Report* 75.

Central Intelligence Agency. 2007. *World Factbook 2006.* Date Retrieved: March 27, 2006. https://www.cia.gov/library/publications/download/download-2006/index.html.

Chaves, M. 1999. "Religious congregations and welfare reform: Who will take advantage of charitable choice?" *American Sociological Review* 64: 836-46.

Chaves, M. 2001. "Religious congregations and welfare reform." *Society* 38: 21-7.

Clear, Todd and George Cole. 1992. *American Corrections, 2nd edition*. Pacific Grove, CA: Brooks/Cole.

Clear, Todd and Edward Latessa. 1993. "Intensive supervision: Surveillance versus treatment." *Justice Quarterly* 10:441–459.

Clear, Todd and David Karp. 1998. *The Community Justice Ideal: Preventing Crime and Achieving Justice.* Westview Press: Boulder, C.O.

Clear, Todd and D. Rose. 1999. *When neighbors go to jail: Impact on attitudes about formal and informal social control.* Washington, DC: National Institute of Justice.

Clear, Todd and R. Corbett. 1999. "Community corrections of place." *Perspectives 23*:24-32.

Clear, T., D. Rose and J. Ryder. 2001. "Incarceration and the Community: The Problem of Removing and Returning Offenders." *Crime and Delinquency 47*:3, 335-351.

Clear, T., D. Rose, and J. Ryder. 2001. "Incarceration and the community: The problem of removing and returning offenders." *Crime and Delinquency 47*, 335-351.

Clear, T. and M. Sumter. 2002. "Prisoners, Prison, and Religion: Religion and Adjustment to Prison." *Journal of Offender Rehabilitation*. 35(3-4):127-59.

Cox, D. 1972. "Regression models and life tables." *Journal of the Royal Statistical Society* 34:187-220.

Cullari, S. 1996. *Treatment Resistance*. Boston: Allyn and Bacon.

Cullen, Francis and Paul Gendreau. 2000. "Assessing Correctional Rehabilitation: Policy, Practice, and Prospects," in *NIJ Criminal Justice 2000: Changes in Decision Making and Discretion in the Criminal Justice System*. Washington, D.C.: U.S. Department of Justice. National Institute of Justice.

Cunniff, Mark. 1991. *Variations on felony probation persons: under supervision in 32 urban and suburban counties*. National Association of Criminal Justice Planners.

Dillon, Paula. 1999. *Special Report: Mental Health and Treatment of Inmates and Probationers*. Washington, D.C.: Office of Justice Programs. Bureau of Justice Statistics.

Ditton, Paula and Doris Wilson. 1999. *Truth in Sentencing in State Prisons*. U.S. Department of Justice. Washington, DC: Bureau of Justice Statistics.

Dowell, D., C. Klein and C. Krichmar. 1985. "Evaluation of a halfway house." *Journal of Criminal Justice 13*, 217-226.

Drug Sense. *The Drug War Clock*. Date Retrieved: January 19, 2010. http://www.drugsense.org/wodclock.htm.

Farabee, D., M. Prendergast, and M. Anglin. 1998. The effectiveness of coerced treatment for drug-abusing offenders. *Federal Probation 62*, 3-10.

Farabee, D., M. Prendergast, J. Cartier, H. Wexler, K. Knight and M. Anglin. 1999. "Barriers to Implementing Effective Correctional Drug Treatment Programs." *Prison Journal 79*:2:150-163.

Feeley, M. and J. Simon. 1992. The New Penology: Notes on the Emerging of Corrections and Its implications. *Criminology* 30: 4: 449-474.

Fellner, J. and M. Mauer. 1998. *Losing the vote: The impact of felony disenfranchisement laws in the United States.* Washington, DC: Human Rights Watch and The Sentencing Project.

Finn, Peter. 1998. *Successful job Placement for Ex-Offenders: The Center for Employment Opportunities Series.* Washington, DC: U.S. Department of Justice. National Institute of Justice.

Finn, Peter. 1999. *Washington State's corrections clearinghouse: A comprehensive approach to offender employment.* Washington, DC: National Institute of Justice.

Gaes, G., T. Flanagan, L. Motiiuk, and L. Stewart. 1999. "Adult correctional treatment." In M. Tonry and J. Petersilia (eds.) *Prisons.* Chicago: University of Chicago Press: 361-426.

Garland, David. 2001. *The Culture of Control: Crime and Social Order in Contemporary Society.* Chicago: The University of Chicago Press.

Gendreau, Paul. 1995. "The Principles of Effective Intervention with Offenders." In Alan Harland (ed.) *Choosing Correctional Options that Work.* Newbury Park, CA: Sage Publications.

Gendreau, Paul. 1996. "Offender Rehabilitation: What We Know and What Needs To Be Done." *Criminal Justice and Behavior*, 23, 144-161.

Gendreau, Paul. and Robert Ross. 1979. "Effective correctional treatment: Bibliotherapy for cynics." *Crime and Delinquency* 25:463-489.

Gendreau, P., T. Little, and C. Goggin. 1996. "Meta-analysis of the predictors of adult offender recidivism: What works?" *Criminology 34:*575-607.

General Accounting Office. 2000. *Education as Crime Prevention: The Case for Reinstating Pell Grant Eligibility for the Incarcerated*. Date Retrieved February 18, 2006. http://www.bard.edu/bpi/pdfs/crime_report.pdf.

Glaze, Lauren. 2003. *Probation and Parole in the United States, 2002*. U.S. Department of Justice. Washington, DC: Bureau of Justice Statistics.

Glaze, Lauren and Thomas Bonczar. 1999. *Correctional Populations in the United States, 1998*. U.S. Department of Justice. Bureau of Justice Statistics.

Glaze, Lauren and Seri Palla. 2004. *Probation and parole in the United States, 2003*. U.S. Department of Justice. Washington, DC: Bureau of Justice Statistics.

Glaze, Lauren and Seri Palla. 2005. *Probation and Parole in the United States, 2004*. U.S. Department of Justice. Washington, DC: Bureau of Justice Statistics.

Glaze, Lauren and Thomas Bonczar. 2006. *Probation and Parole in the United States, 2005*. U.S. Department of Justice. Washington, DC: Bureau of Justice Statistics.

Goldstein, P. J. 1985. "The drugs/violence nexus: A tripartite conceptual framework." *Journal of Drug Issues*, *15*(4): 493-506.

Gottfredson, S. and R. Taylor. 1986. "Person-Environment Interactions in the Prediction of Recidivism." in J. Byrne and R. Sampson (eds) *The Social Ecology of Crime*. New York: Springer-Verlag.

Gottfredson, M. and T. Hirschi. 1990. *A General Theory of Crime*. CT: Stanford University.

Greene, Judith and Kevin Pranis. 2006. *Treatment instead of Prisons: A Roadmap for Sentencing and Correctional Policy Reform*. Justice Strategies and the Drug Policy Alliance.

Hagan, John and Ronit Dinovitzer. 1999. "Collateral Consequences of Imprisonment for Children, Communities, and Prisoners." In M. Tonry and J. Petersilia (eds.) *Prisons*. Chicago: University of Chicago Press.

Hammett, T., S. Roberts and S. Kennedy. 2001. "Health-Related Issues in Prisoner Reentry to the Community." *Crime and Delinquency* 47: 3, 390-409.

Hammett, T., J. Gaiter, and C. Crawford. 1998. "Reaching seriously at-risk populations: Health interventions in criminal justice settings." *Health Education and Behavior 25*:99-120.

Hammett, T., C. Roberts, and S. Kennedy. 2002. "Health-Related Issues in Prisoner Reentry." *Crime and Delinquency* 47(3):390–409.

Harer, Miles. 1994. *Recidivism of Federal Prisoners Released in 1987.* Washington, D.C.: Federal Bureau of Prisons, Office of Research and Evaluation.

Harlow, C.J. 2003. *Education and Correctional Populations.* U.S. Department of Justice. Washington, D.C.: Bureau of Justice Statistics.

Harrison, Lana. 2001. "The Revolving Prison Door for Drug-Involved Offenders: Challenges and Opportunities." *Crime and Delinquency*, Vol. 47, No. 3, 462-485.

Harrison, Paige. and Allen Beck. 2002. *Prisoners in 2001.* U.S. Department of Justice. Washington, DC: Bureau of Justice Statistics.

Harrison, Paige and Allen Beck. 2003. *Prisoners in 2002.* Washington, D.C.: U.S. Department of Justice. Bureau of Justice Statistics.

Harrison, Paige and Allen Beck. 2004. *Prisoners in 2003.* U.S. Department of Justice. Washington, DC: Bureau of Justice Statistics.

Harrison, Paige and Jennifer Karberg. 2004. *Prison and jail inmates at midyear 2003.* U.S. Department of Justice. Washington, DC: Bureau of Justice Statistics.

Harrison, Paige. and Jennifer Karberg. 2005. *Prison and Jail Inmates at Midyear 2004.* U.S. Department of Justice. Washington, DC: Bureau of Justice Statistics.

Helzer, J. and T. Pryzbeck. 1988. "The co-occurrence of alcoholism with other psychiatric disorders in the general population and its impact on treatment." *Journal of Studies on Alcohol* 49:219–224.

Hiller, M. K. Knight and D. Simpson. 1999. "Prison Based Substance Abuse Treatment, Residential Aftercare and Recidivism." *Addiction* 94(6):833-842.

Hirschi, Travis and Rodney Stark. 1969. "Hellfire and Delinquency." *Social Problems*, 17: 202-213.

Hoffman, P. and A. Beck. 1985. "Recidivism among released federal prisoners: Salient factor score and five year follow-up." *Criminal Justice and Behavior* 12:501–507.

Hoffmann, N., J. Halikas, D. Mee-Lee and R. Weedman. 1991. *Patient Placement Criteria for the Treatment of Psychoactive Substance Use Disorders.* Washington, D.C: American Society of Addiction Medicine.

Hughes, T. and D. Wilson. 2003. *Reentry Trends in the United States.*

U.S. Department of Justice. Washington, D.C.: Bureau of Justice Statistics.

Hughes, T., D. Wilson and A. Beck. 2001. *Trends in State Parole, 1990–2000.* U.S. Department of Justice. Washington, DC: Bureau of Justice Statistics.

Inciardi, J., S. Martin, and C. Butzin. 2004. "Five-year outcomes of therapeutic community treatment of drug-involved offenders after release from prison." *Crime and Delinquency 50*(1):88-107.

Inciardi, J. S. Martin, C.Butzin, R. Hooper and L.Harrison. 1997. "An effective model of prison-based treatment for drug-involved offenders." *Journal of Drug Issues 27*(2):261-278.

Johnson, B. 2001. "Reviewing and Clarifying the Role of Religion in Reducing Crime and Delinquency." *Federal Probation.* 65(3):49-53.

Johnson, B., R. Tompkins and D. Webb. 2002. Objective Hope: Assessing the Effectiveness of Faith-Based Organizations: A Review of the Literature. CRRUS Report.

Johnson, B.R. 1984. *Hellfire and Corrections: A Quantitative Study of Florida Prison Inmates.* Doctoral Dissertation, Florida State University.

Knight, K., D. Simpson, and M. Hiller. 2002. "Screening and referral for substance-abuse treatment in the criminal justice system." In C. G.

Leukefeld, F. Tims, and D. Farabee , *Treatment of drug offenders: Policies and issues*. New York: Springer.

Koyanagi, Chris, 2002. *Finding the Key to Successful Transition from Jail to the Community*. Washington, D.C.: Bazelon Center for Mental Health Law.

Lake City. 2003. Grant Proposal Submitted on Behalf of Lake City for Faith based Community Based Treatment." Governor of the State's Office.

Landis, J., J. Mercer and C. Wolff. 1969. "Success and Failure of Adult Probationers in California." *Journal of Research in Crime and Delinquency* 6(1):34-40.

Langan P. and M. Cunniff. 1992. *Recidivism of felons on probation, 1986-1989*. U.S. Department of Justice. Washington, DC: Bureau of Justice Statistics.

Langan, Patrick and David Levin. 2002. *Recidivism of Prisoners Released in 1994*. U.S. Department of Justice. Washington, DC: Bureau of Justice Statistics.

Langan, P., E. Schmitt, and M. Durose. 2003. *Recidivism of Sex Offenders Released from Prison in 1994*. Washington, D.C.: U.S. Department of Justice. Bureau of Justice Statistics.

Lattimore, P., J. Baker, and E. Clayton 2000. "A Nonlinear Multiple Criteria Model Base for the Problem of Balancing Caseload Risk in Probation Departments." *Computers and Industrial Engineering: An International Journal* 35(4):511-514.

Lattimore, P., S. Brumbaugh, C. Visher, C. Lindquist, L. Winterfield, M. Salas. 2004. *National portrait of SVORI.* Charlotte, NC: Research Triangle Park, RTI International.

Lattimore, P., J. MacDonald, A. Piquero, R. Linster, and C. Visher. 2004. "Studying the Characteristics of Arrest Frequency among Paroled Youthful Offenders." *Journal of Research in Crime and Delinquency* 41(1):37-57.

Laub, John and Robert Sampson. 2001. "Desistence from Crime." Crime and Justice 28:1-69.

Laub, John, and Robert Sampson. 2003. *Shared Beginnings, Divergent Lives: Delinquent Boys to age 70.* Cambridge: Harvard University Press.

Leonhard, C., K. Mulvey, D. Gastfriend, M. Schwartz and H. Wei. 2000. "The addiction severity index: A field study of reliability and validity." *Journal of Substance Abuse Treatment* 18:129-135.

Leshner, A. I. 1998. "Drug addiction research: Moving toward the 21st century." *Drug and Alcohol Dependence* 51:5–7.

Lipton, D., R. Martinson, and J. Wilks. 1975. *The effectiveness of correctional treatment: A survey of treatment evaluation studies.* New York: Praeger.

Lipton, D., F. Pearson and H. Wexler. 2000. *Final report: National evaluation of the Residential Substance Abuse Treatment for state prisoners program from onset to midpoint.* Washington, DC: National Institute of Justice.

Longshore, D., S. Turner, and T. Fain. 2005. "Effects of case management on parolee misconduct: The Bay Area Services Network." *Criminal Justice and Behavior* 25(2): 422-435.

Lurigio, A. J. 1996. *Community corrections in America: New directions and sounder investments for persons with mental illness and co-disorders.* Seattle, WA: National Coalition for Mental and Substance Abuse Health Care in the Justice System.

Lynch, James and William Sabol. 2001. "Prisoner Reentry in Perspective." *Crime Policy Report Vol. 3*. Washington, D.C.: Urban Institute Press.

MacKenzie, D. and S. De Li. 2002. "The impact of formal and informal social controls on the criminal activities of probationers." *Journal of research in crime and delinquency* 39(3):243-276.

MacKenzie, Doris. 1997. "Criminal justice and crime prevention" in Sherman, LW, *et al.*(eds) *What works, what doesn't, what's promising*. University of Maryland.

MacKenzie, D. and L. Hickman. 1998. *What Works in Corrections?* Report to the State of Washington Legislature Joint Audit and Review Subcommittee.

Maguire, K. and A. Pastore. 1997. *Sourcebook of Criminal Justice Statistics 1996*. Washington, DC: U.S. Department of Justice.

Mäkelä, K. 2004. "Studies of the reliability and validity of the Addiction Severity Index." *Addiction* 99:398-410.

Maltz, Michael. 1984. *Recidivism.* New York: Academic Press.

Martin, S. and J. Inciardi. 1993. "A case management treatment program for drug-involved prison releases." *The Prison Journal* 73:319-331.

Martin, S., C. Butzin, C. Saum, and J. Inciardi. 1999. "Three-year outcomes of therapeutic community treatment for drug involved offenders in Delaware: from prison to work release to aftercare." *The Prison Journal.* 79(3):294-320.

Martinson, Robert. 1974. "What works? Questions and answers about prison reform." *Public Interest 35*:22-45.

Martinson, Robert. 1979. "New findings, new reviews: A note of caution regarding sentencing reform." *Hofstra Law Review 7*:243-258.

Maruschak, L. and A. Beck. 2001. *Medical problems of inmates, 1997.* U.S. Department of Justice. Washington, DC: Bureau of Justice Statistics.

Maxfield, M. and E. Babbie. 2006. *Research Methods for Criminal Justice and Criminology, 5th edtion*. Belmont, CA: Thomson Wadsworth.

Mauer, Mark. 2001. "The Causes and Consequences of Prison Growth in the United States." *Punishment and Society* 3(1):9-20.

McGahan, P., J. Griffith, R. Parente and T. McClellan. 1986. ASI Composite Score Manual. National Institute of Drug Abuse. Philadelphia, PA: Treatment Research Institute.

McLellan, A. and G. Woody. 1998. *Evaluating the effectiveness of treating drug abusers effectively*. Malden, MA: Blackwell Publishers.

McLellan, A., T. Luborsky and C. O'Brien, 1982. "Is treatment for substance abuse effective?" *Journal of the American Medical Association*. 247(10):1423-1428.

Métraux, Steven and Dennis Culhane. 2004. "Homeless shelter use and reincarceration following prison release: Assessing the risk." *Criminology and Public Policy* 3(2):201-222.

Mumola, Christopher. 1999. *Substance Abuse and Treatment, State and Federal Prisoners, 1997*. U.S. Department of Justice. Washington, DC: Bureau of Justice Statistics.

Mumola, Christopher. 2000. *Incarcerated parents and their children*. U.S. Department of Justice. Washington, DC: Bureau of Justice Statistics.

National Advisory Commission on Criminal Justice Standards and Goals. 1973. *Task Force Report on Corrections*. Washington, DC: Government Printing Office.

National Association of State Budget Officers (NASBO). 2004. *The Fiscal Survey of States*. National Governor's Association.

National Commission on Correctional Health Care. 2002. *The Health Status of Soon to be released Inmates: A Report to Congress*. U.S. Department of Justice. Washington, DC: National Institute of Justice.

National Institute on Drug Abuse (NIDA). 1999. *Principles of drug addiction treatment*. Rockville, MD: National Institutes of Health.

National Institute on Drug Abuse (NIDA). 2000. *Principles of Drug Addiction Treatment.* Rockville, MD: National Institute of Health.

National Institute of Justice. 2000. *2000 Arrestee Drug Abuse Monitoring: Annual Report*. U.S. Department of Justice. Washington, DC: Arrestee Drug Abuse Monitoring Program (ADAM).

Nelson, M., Deess, P., and Allen, C. 1999. *The First Month Out: Post-Incarceration Experiences in New York City*. New York: Vera Institute of Justice.

Nurco, D. N. 1998. "A long term program of research on drug use and crime." *Substance Use and Misuse* 33(9):1817-1838.

O'Brien, C., and T. McClelland. 1996. "Myths about the treatment of addiction." *Lancet* 347, 237-240.

O'Connor, Thomas, Yang Su, Patricia Ryan, Crystal Parikh and Estrelda Alexander. 1997. *Detroit Transition of Prisoners: Final Evaluation Report*. Silver Spring, MD: Center for Social Research 1–25.

Office of National Drug Control Policy. 2003. *Fiscal Year 2004 Budget Summary.* Washington, DC: National Drug Control Strategy Committee.

Oliver, Pamela. *Racial Disparities in Criminal Justice.* Date Retrieved June16, 2006: http://www.ssc.wisc.edu/~oliver/racial/racialdisparities.html.

Pager, Devah. 2003. "The mark of a criminal record." *American Journal of Sociology* 108:937-975.

Patton, Wesley. 1990. "The world where parallel lines converge: The privilege against self-incrimination in concurrent civil and criminal child abuse proceedings." *Georgia Law Review* 24(3):473-524.

Pearson, F. and D. Lipton. 1999. "A meta-analytic review of the effectiveness of corrections based treatments for drug abuse." *The Prison Journal 79*(4):384-410.

Peters, R. and M. Murrin. 2000. "Effectiveness of treatment-based drug courts in reducing criminal recidivism." *Criminal Justice and Behavior 20(*1):72-96.

Petersilia, Joan. 1985. "Community supervision: Trends and critical issues." *Crime and Delinquency 31*:339-347.

Petersilia, Joan. 1998. "Probation and parole." In M Tonry (ed). *The Handbook of Crime and Punishment.* New York: Oxford University Press.

Petersilia, Joan. 1999. "Parole and prisoner reentry in the United States." In M. Tonry and J. Petersilia (eds). *Prisons.* Chicago, IL: The University of Chicago Press.

Petersilia, Joan. 2001. "Prisoner reentry: Public safety and reintegration challenges." *The Prison Journal* 81(3):360-375.

Petersilia, Joan. 2004a. "What Works in Prisoner Reentry? Reviewing and Questioning the Evidence." *Federal Probation 68*:4-8.

Petersilia, Joan. 2004b. *"When Prisoners Come Home: Parole and Prisoner Reentry.* Oxford, UK: Oxford University Press.

Petersilia, J. and S. Turner. 1993. "Intensive probation and parole." In Michael Tonry , *Crime and justice: A review of research*. Chicago: University of Chicago Press.

Petersilia, J. and J. Travis. 2001. "Reentry Reconsidered: A New Look at an Old Question." *Crime and Delinquency* 47(3):291-313.

PEW Charitable Trusts. 2008. *One in 100: America Behind Bars 2008*. http://www. Pewcenteronthestates.org/.

PEW Charitable Trusts. 2007. *Public Safety and Public Spending: Operating and Capital Expenditures from 2007-2011*. http://www. Pewcenteronthestates.org/.

Piliavin, I., B. Wright, R. Mare and A. Westerfelt. 1996. "Exits and returns to homelessness." *Social Service Review* 70(1):33-57.

Polizzi, D., D. MacKenzie and J. Hickman. 1999. "What works in adult sex offender treatment? A review of prison and non-prison based treatment programs." *International Journal of Offender Therapy and Comparative Criminology 43*(3):357-374.

Prendergast, M., J. Wellisch, and G. Falkin. 1995. "Assessment of and services for substance-abusing women offenders in community and correctional settings." *The Prison Journal 75*:240-256.

Prendergast, M., D. Farabee, J. Cartier, H.Wexler, K. Knight and M. Anglin. 1999. "Barriers to Implementing Effective Correctional Drug Treatment Programs." *The Prison Journal* 79(2).

RAND Corporation. 2003. "Prisoner Reentry: What are the Public Health Challenges?" *Rand Research Brief.* Santa Monica, CA: RAND Public and Safety Justice.

Rhine, E. and M. Paparozzi. 1999. "Reinventing Probation and Parole: A Matter of Consequence." *Corrections Management Quarterly* 32:47-52.

Rhodes, W., B.Pelissier, G. Gaes, W. Saylor, S. Camp, and S. Wallace. 2001. "Alternative solutions to the problem of selection bias in an analysis of federal residential drug treatment programs." *Evaluation Review 25*(3):331-369.

Riley, John. 2003. "Freed Into Limbo: Laws, Lack of Preparation Leave Ex-Cons Struggling to Stay Straight." *Newsday*, August 3, 2003.

Robinson, L., and J. Travis. 2005. Managing prisoner reentry for public safety. Unpublished manuscript.

Roman, C. and J. Travis. 2004. *Taking Stock: Housing, Homelessness and Prisoner Reentry*. Bethesda. MD: The Urban Institute.

Rosenthal, Alan and Elaine Wolf. 2004. *Unlocking the potential of reentry and reintegration: A Reintegrative Sentencing model.* Retrieved July 19, 2007. http://www.communityalternatives.org/pdfs/unlocking_potential.pdf

Rothman, David. 1971. *The discovery of the asylum: Social order and disorder in the new republic*. Boston, MA: Little Brown

Sabol, W., T. Minton and P. Harrison. 2007. *Prison and Jail Inmates at Midyear 2006.* U.S. Department of Justice. Washington, DC: Bureau of Justice Statistics.

Sard, B. and M. Waller. 2002. *Housing Strategies to Strengthen Welfare Policy and Support Working Families.* Washington, D.C.: The Brookings Institution.

Schlay, A. and P Rossi. 1992. "Social science research and contemporary studies of homelessness." *Annual Review of Sociology* 18:129-16.

Siefert, K. and S. Pimlott. 2001. "Improving pregnancy outcome during imprisonment: a model residential care program." *Social Work 46*(2):125-134.

Seiter, R. P. (1975). *Evaluation research as a feedback mechanism for criminal justice policy making: A critical analysis*. Unpublished dissertation. Columbus: Ohio State University.

Seiter, R. and K. Kadela. 2003. "Prisoner Reentry: What Works, What Does Not, and What is Promising." *Crime and Delinquency* 49(3):360-388.

Shadish, W., T. Cook, and D. Campbell. 2002. *Experimental and Quasi-Experimental Designs for Generalized Causal Inference*. Boston: Houghton Mifflin.

Sherman, Lawrence. 1999. *Evidence-based policing. Ideas in American policing*. Washington, DC: The Police Foundation.

Sherman, L., D. Gottfredson, D. MacKenzie, J. Eck, P. Reuter and S. Bushway. 1997. *Preventing crime: What works, what doesn't, what's promising*. College Park: University of Maryland Press.

Simpson J., D. Dwayne, H. Wexler and J. Inciardi. 1999. "Drug Treatment Outcomes for Correctional Settings, Part 1." *The Prison Journal 79:3*: 291-293.

Sims, B. and M. Jones. 1997. "Predicting success or failure on probation: Factors associated with felony probation outcomes." *Crime and Delinquency 43*:314-327.

Singer, M., J. Bussey, L. Song and L. Lungerhofer. 1995. "The psychosocial issue of women serving time in jail." *Social Work* 40:103-113.

Sorensen, J. L., J. Dilley, J. London, R. Okin, K. Delucchi, and C. Phibbs. 2003. "Case management for substance abusers with HIV/AIDS: A randomized clinical trial." *The American Journal of Drug and Alcohol Abuse 29*(1):133-150.

State Court System. *Yearend Disposition Summary: Statewide Report*. State Court System Database. Date Retrieved: December 11, 2006.

State Department of Corrections. 2005. *Offenders Under Control on December 30, 2005*." Date Retrieved: November 11, 2006.

State Department of Corrections. 2004a. *FY2004: Preliminary State Budget Expenditures*. Date Retrieved: January, 2006.

State Department of Corrections. 2004b. *Offenders Released Statewide*. Date Retrieved: January, 2006.

State Sentencing Commission. 2002. State Subcommittee: Reporting on Statewide Offenders Released From Prison. Date Retrieved: March 17, 2006.

Steurer, S., L. Smith and A. Tracy. 2001. *Three State Recidivism Study*. Correctional Education Association. The United States Department of Education's Office of Correctional Education: 1–2.

Stojkovic, S., R.Lovell and S. Brandl. 2003. *Felony Drug Offender Alternative to Prison Program Final Report*. Lake City University Press.

Substance Abuse and Mental Health Services Administration (SAMHSA). 2006. *Access To Recovery Programming*. Date Retrieved January 11, 2006: http://atr.samhsa.gov/AggregateDataProfiles.aspx.

Substance Abuse and Mental Health Services Administration (SAMSHA). 1999. *The relationship between mental health and substance abuse among Adolescents*. Rockville, MD: Substance Abuse and Mental Health Services Administration.

Sumter, Melvina. 2006. "Faith based Prison Programs." *Criminology and Public Policy* 5(3):523–528.

Taxman, Faye. 1998. "12 Steps to Improved Offender Outcomes: Developing Responsive Systems of Care for Substance-Abusing Offenders." *Corrections Today*, *60*:6, 114-117.

Taxman, Faye. 1999. "Unraveling What Works for Offenders in Substance Abuse Treatment Services." *National Drug Court Institute Review, Vol. II*, 2: 93-134.

Taxman, F. and R. Cherkos. 1995. "Intermediate sanctions: Dealing with technical violators." *Corrections Today*, 57, 46-57.

Taxman, F.. D. Young, J. Byrne, A. Holsinger and D. Anspach. 2002. *From Prison to Public Safety: Innovations in Offender Reentry*. Rockville, MD: National Institute of Justice.

Taxman, F., D. Young and J. Byrne. 2003a. *Offenders View of Reentry: Implications for Processes, Programs, and Services*. Washington, D.C.: National Institute of Justice.

Taxman, F., J. Byrne and D. Young. 2003b. *Targeting for reentry: Matching needs and services to maximize public safety*. Washington, DC: National Institute of Justice.

Taxman, F., D. Young and J. Byrne. 2004. "Transforming offender reentry into public safety: Lessons from the Office of Justice Program's Reentry Partnership Initiative." *Justice Policy and Research* 5:101-128.

The Sentencing Project. 2004. *Incarceration Statistics Across States*. Date Retrieved: November 11, 2004: http://www.sentencingproject.org/StatsByState.aspx.

Tonry, Michael. 1998. *The Handbook of Crime and Punishment*. New York: Oxford University Press.

Tonry, Michael and James Wilson. 1990. *Drugs and crime*. Chicago: University of Chicago Press.

Travis, Jeremy. 2000. *But they all come back: Rethinking prisoner reentry*. Washington, DC: National Institute of Justice.

Travis, J. and S. Lawrence. 2002. *Beyond the Prison Gates: The State of Parole in America.* Washington, DC: The Urban Institute.

Travis, J. and J. Petersilia, 2003. "Reentry Reconsidered: A New Look at an Old Question." *Crime and Delinquency* 47:3.

Travis, J., A. Solomon and M. Waul. 2001. *From Prison to Home: The Dimensions and Consequences of Prisoner Reentry*. Washington, DC: The Urban Institute.

Travis, J., A. Solomon and M. Waul. 2003. *A Portrait of Prisoner Reentry in Maryland.* Washington, DC: The Urban Institute.

Travis, J., E. Cincotta and A. Solomon. 2003. *Families Left Behind: The Hidden Costs of Incarceration and Reentry*. Washington, DC: The Urban Institute.

Uggen, Christopher. 2000. "Work as a turning point in the life course of criminals: A duration model of age, employment, and recidivism." *American Sociological Review* 67:529-546.

Unknown Author. 2004. "Crime and Corrections." *The State Taxpayer* 72: 9.

U.S. Conference of Mayors. 2002. *A Status Report on Hunger and Homelessness in American Cities, 2002.* Washington, DC: United States Conference of Mayors.

Vidal, Avis. 2001. *Faith based Organizations in Community Development.* Report prepared for U.S. Department of

Housing and Community Development. Office of Policy Development and Research.

Vigilante, K., M. Flynn, P. Affleck, J. Stunkle, N. Merriman, T. Flanigan, J. Mitty and J. Rich. 1999. "Reduction in Recidivism of incarcerated women through primary care, peer counseling, and discharge planning." *Journal of Women's Health* 8:409-415.

Visher, C. and N. LaVigne. 2003. *Returning Home: Understanding the Challenges of Prisoner Reentry: Maryland Pilot Study: Findings from Baltimore.* Washington D.C.: The Urban Institute.

Visher, C., N. LaVigne, and J. Farrell. 2003. *Illinois Prisoners' Reflections on Returning Home.* Washington, D.C.: The Urban Institute.

Visher, C., N. Kachnowski, N. La Vigne, and J. Travis. 2004. *Baltimore Prisoners' Experiences Returning Home.* Washington, DC: The Urban Institute.

Vito, G. and R. Tewksbury. 1999. "Improving the Educational Skills of Jail Inmates: The Results of an Impact Evaluation." *Corrections Compendium* 24(10):11-18.

Walker, S., C. Spohn and M. DeLone. 2008. *The Color of Justice, 5th edition.* San Francisco, CA.: Wadsworth Publishing.

Walmsley, Roy. 2006. *Prison Population List, 6th Edition.* London, UK: King's College: International Center for Prison Studies.

Weiss, Carol. 1998. *Evaluation: Methods for Studying Programs and Policies, 2nd Edition.* Upper Saddle River, N.J: Prentice-Hall.

Welch, K. and M. Quirke. 2002. *Substance Abuse Treatment Capacity Analysis: 2000.* City within State: Department of Health and Family Services. Bureau of Mental Health and Substance Abuse Services.

Welch, K. and M. Quirke. 2005. *Substance Abuse Treatment Needs, Capacity and Costs: 2003.* City within State:

Department of Health and Family Services. Bureau of Mental Health and Substance Abuse Services.

Western, B. and B. Pettit. 2000. "Incarceration and Racial Inequality in.Men's Employment." *Industrial and Labor Relations Review* 54:3-16.

Western, B.,J. Kling and D. Weiman. 2001. "The Labor Market Consequences of Incarceration." *Crime and Delinquency* (47):410-27.

Wilcox, Pamela. 1998. "A reexamination of the crime-fear linkage." *Journal of Research in Crime and Delinquency* 35:341-372.

Wilson, James. 2000. *Crime: Public Policies for Crime Control, 2nd edition*. Oakland, CA: ICS Press.

Workman, Kim. 2005. Recent Research Supporting the Underlying Theories of APAC-Based Prisons. Prison Fellowship of New Zealand. Date Retrieved: June 21, 2007. http://www.pfnz.org.nz/publications/research.htm.

Young, D. 1998. "Health status and service use among incarcerated women." *Journal of Prison Jail Health 10*:43-57.

Zhang, Z. 2004. *Drug and alcohol use and related matters among arrestees, 2003*. U.S. Department of Justice. Washington, DC: National Institute of Justice.

Zimring, F. and G. Hawkins. 1995. *Incapacitation: Penal confinement and restraint of Crime*. Oxford: Oxford University Press.

Index